Young Writers 2005 POE

PLAYGROUN

Let your creativity flow...

ode
limerick haiku
rhyme

- Inspirations From
London Vol III
Edited by Bobby Tobolik

 Young **Writers**

First published in Great Britain in 2006 by:
Young Writers
Remus House
Coltsfoot Drive
Peterborough
PE2 9JX
Telephone: 01733 890066
Website: www.youngwriters.co.uk

SB ISBN 1 84602 344 0

Foreword

Young Writers was established in 1991 and has been passionately devoted to the promotion of reading and writing in children and young adults ever since. The quest continues today. Young Writers remains as committed to the fostering of burgeoning poetic and literary talent as ever.

This year's Young Writers competition has proven as vibrant and dynamic as ever and we are delighted to present a showcase of the best poetry from across the UK. Each poem has been carefully selected from a wealth of *Playground Poets* entries before ultimately being published in this, our thirteenth primary school poetry series.

Once again, we have been supremely impressed by the overall high quality of the entries we have received. The imagination, energy and creativity which has gone into each young writer's entry made choosing the best poems a challenging and often difficult but ultimately hugely rewarding task - the general high standard of the work submitted amply vindicating this opportunity to bring their poetry to a larger appreciative audience.

We sincerely hope you are pleased with our final selection and that you will enjoy *Playground Poets - Inspirations From London Vol III* for many years to come.

Contents

Joy Princess Gardiner (9)	32
Tashana Nelson (9)	32
Mine Kizilkaya (9)	33
Mihriban Kinik & Rodi Kurt (9)	33
Corey Powell-Strachan & Nada Loudiyi (8)	33
Shane-Curtis Hines (8)	34
Melissa Roberts (10)	34
Georja Matthew & Ella Stephen-Oladele (8)	34
Afua Agyeman (8)	35
Lorita Abazi & Helin Dogan (8)	35
Demi Spencer (10)	35
Afua Agyeman & Lateschar Tyrell (8)	36
Jennifer De Oliveria & Savannah (8)	36

Gordonbrock Primary School, Brockley

Haleema Nazir (7)	36
Jessica Eschoe-Naylor (8)	37
Maia Okoloba (7)	37
Rhiannon Miller-Douglas (8)	38
Moya Biggs Teiona (9)	38
Layla Saleemi (8)	39
Hazel Dawson (8)	39
Anisa Mohammed (8)	40
Mignone Aina (8)	40
Hawa Ali (7)	40
Lauren Harris (9)	41
Kwadwo Kankam (8)	41
Zachary Alamir Quallo (8)	42
Amber Lawrence (8)	42
Fatih Gök (8)	43
Ceykan Ramadan (9)	43
Dhilon Selvaratnam (8)	44
Ronnie Tharme	44
Megan Gosnell (8)	45
Zekiye Hamit (9)	45
Benjamin White (8)	46
Milo Harper (8)	46
Georgia South (8)	47
Ella Elizabeth Puttick (8)	47
Jasmin Winifred (8)	48
Siân Ella Keogh (8)	48

Emmanuel Park (7)	73
Charlie Joseph Carney (8)	74
Jason Jouan (10)	74
Theo Johns (8)	75
Aaron Akpojaro (7)	76
Liam Cavanagh (8)	77
Shareen Ffrench (10)	77
Kitty Walker (8)	78
Stephanie Hilbig (8)	79
Stephany Hernandez (9)	80
Chloe Sandley	80
Laura Burns (7)	81
John Costello (10)	82
Susan Uwah (10)	82
Jessie Grace Cooney (10)	83
Natasha Adomako (10)	84
Ronnie Odlum (10)	84
Milly Odlum (8)	85
Sean Fowley (10)	86
Hannah Louise Smith (10)	87
Kieran Cavanagh (10)	88
Olamide Somade (10)	89
Jessica Ball (10)	90
Leanne Gale King (10)	90
Sam Mills (10)	91
Jordan Akpojaro (11)	91
Ann-Marie Whelan (9)	92
Thomas Hilbig (10)	93
Katie-Louise Shepherd Gill (10)	93
Mitchell Roy Burns (10)	94
Jessica Baxter (9)	95
Shannon Edwards (7)	95
Paige Holdaway (9)	96
Callum Fransen (10)	97
Chelsey-Ann Yousif (10)	98
Pearle Morha (8)	99
Samantha Tuckey	100
Ruairi O'Connor (9)	101
Jack Amphlett (10)	102
Benjamin Samuel (9)	103
Jack Trype (8)	104
Lydia Agui (7)	105

Oxford Gardens Primary School, Oxford Gardens

Rainbow Montessori School, West Hampstead

St Andrew's RC Primary School, Streatham

St Anthony's RC Primary School, Dulwich

St Joseph's RC School, Hanwell

St Joseph's RC School, Willesden

Katie O'Keeffe (9)	193
Gabriella Diaferia (9)	193
Michelle Karlsson (9)	194
Jessie Chan (8)	194
Daisy Francis (9)	195
Kiki Biggs (9)	195
Mona Hickey (9)	196
Cecilia Tyrrell (9)	196
Amelia Seifalian (9)	196
Charlotte Dougall (9)	197
Eloise Donovan (9)	197
Katherine Lampard (10)	198
Millie Barber (9)	198
Phoebe Mallett (9)	198
Iona Nicolson (10)	199
Constance Osborne (9)	199

St Peter's Primary School, Hammersmith

Ruby Mercer (9)	200
Lily Biddell (9)	200
Babette Van Gerwen (9)	201
Sam Eccles (10)	201
Megan Gerrard (9)	202
Ngozi Diamond (9)	202
Sam Smith (9)	203
Emma Grace (9)	203
Keri Rothwell-Douglas (9)	204
Obi Raphael (9)	204
Leila Tompkins (9)	205
Jack Gibbon (9)	205
Mia Fennimore Holdsworth (9)	206
Iona Stirling (9)	207
Rosie Morgan (9)	208
Louis Earle (9)	208
Wallis Gray (9)	209
Edward Thorpe-Woods (9)	209
Bert Azis-Clauson (9)	210
Alex Burch (10)	211

St Stephen's CE Primary School, Westminster

Sir William Burrough Primary School, Limehouse

Thomas Fairchild Community School, Hackney

The Poems

Kruger Park

It was dark
When we got to the Kruger Park
And up came the sun
And then we had lots of fun.

We heard a big lion roar
Then we saw some elephants
Fall to the floor.

The baboons were in the trees
Eating each other's fleas
And the monkeys were throwing bananas at the
Zebras who were in their stripy pyjamas.

The big grey hippo in the pool
Keeping nice and cool.

When the sun went down
I made a frown and it was time
To get into my dressing gown.

Josephine Cooper (7)
All Saints CE Primary School, Fulham

Tigers

Tigers are scary
They like to eat meat,
They have sharp claws
On the end of their feet.

Tigers live in India,
Where it's hot in the sun,
They watch their prey
In the grass and run.

Tigers live alone,
They like to hunt at night,
If you meet a tiger
You'll get a horrible fright.

Bertie Simpson (7)
All Saints CE Primary School, Fulham

Dads

Sometimes dads are annoying
Also are never cunning
They think they're hysterical
And also think they're a miracle
Once my dad had a coma
And looked exactly like Homer
Dads eat breakfast madly
And clean their teeth badly
My dad eats breakfast with jelly
So now he has a massive belly
My dad is a fan of telly
Now he is very smelly
My dad sings in the shower
So now he has super power
Dads are very weird
So they have the biggest beards
My dad knows French and German
So gets confused when it's his sermon.

That's my dad.

Emma Stilwell (7)
All Saints CE Primary School, Fulham

The Beach

The beach is fun, it is hotter than the sun.
The sun is bright, I fly a kite in the middle of the night,
What a wonderful sight,
I hurt my knees in the sea.
I climbed on the tree and shouted, 'Look at me!'
I found a key in the sea and I got stung by a bee.

So we went to the beach and the day was OK,
But my things got blown away as it was a windy day.

Sophia Shamsi (7)
All Saints CE Primary School, Fulham

Colours Of The Rainbow

Red is the colour of foxes in
their comfortable grassy beds.

Yellow is the colour of the sun
that shines on our heads.

Pink is the colour of a pencil
that you can write or draw with.

Blue is the colour of the sea
that splatters and clatters.

Orange is the colour of an orange
that you can eat.

Green is the colour of the grass
that you play on.

Purple is the colour of my sharpener
that I could sharpen my pencils with.

Caitlin Cox-Groden (7)
All Saints CE Primary School, Fulham

I Have Fun

I sit by my window
Waiting for my mum,
So we can have some fun,
I love having fun with my mum,
When we go to the park
Sometimes we stay until dark,
But when I am naughty
My mum tells me to behave myself
You naughty little Chloe,
I know my mum will
Always be there for me
Because she loves me.

Chloe Anna Danquah (7)
All Saints CE Primary School, Fulham

Cats And Dogs!

C ats are furry
A lways chasing mice
T ails are fluffy

D on't like cats
O h! Run cat run!
G et up that tree and you will be free.

Lulu Delilah Lavall (7)
All Saints CE Primary School, Fulham

Harvest

H arvest time is here once more
A pples and pears to feed the poor
R ice and corn to fill the barns
V egetables and fruits grown in farms
E ach fruit and vegetable that we eat
S uch a nice and healthy treat
T o share with all the people we meet!

Mati Ortiz (7)
All Saints CE Primary School, Fulham

Rinky Dinky Doo

The kangaroo
With a tattoo
Played a didgeridoo
The didgeridoo made a hullaballoo
Mr Cockatoo said, 'Shoo!'

Jasmine Hill (7)
All Saints CE Primary School, Fulham

Autumn

In the autumn when the leaves are falling
and the grass is dew-ridden on the ground.
The berries are juicy and the earth is wet,
and the birds are flying overhead from their nests.
I like playing in the autumn sun, watching
the squirrels run around and the rabbits hopping
in and out of holes, whilst the foxes play in the
woods with the leaves all around.
When the fire is burning and the chimney is
smoking and it is nice and warm inside.
Outside the wind is blowing.
I love autumn.

Fred Beaty (7)
All Saints CE Primary School, Fulham

The Rat And The Cat

My cat sang a song
that went *dong* and
was friends with King Kong
who loved to say, 'Bong,'
in the song that was very long.
My cat had a friend called Bat
who went rat-a-tat-tat and married a rat.
But the rat and the cat weren't good friends,
so they argued all day and night
till they went to Sandy Bay all day.

My cat sat, he was so happy to be a cat
because he could eat rat while he sat.

Lottie Maddocks (7)
All Saints CE Primary School, Fulham

Amazon

A mazon, big and wide
M any birds flying in the sky
A lligator all hungry, bye, swimming under the water looking sly
Z ebras and elephants we can't find here, but anacondas
                                       are very near
O rang-utan, big and hairy, swing through the jungle looking scary
N ever-ending river running through the Amazon beautifully
                               and plants growing wildly.

Ella Ashdown (7)
All Saints CE Primary School, Fulham

Mice

I think mice are rather nice.
They run fast and nibble lots of rice.
They have a browny-grey black fur coat
And their eyes are really small and shiny.
I'd make a trap with some cheese
And snap the trap and that would be
The end of mice.

Harriet Vause (7)
All Saints CE Primary School, Fulham

My Butterfly

Beautiful colour
Pollen lover
Wing flapper
Graceful flier
Quiet mover
My butterfly.

Lottie Gaffney (7)
All Saints CE Primary School, Fulham

Puppies, Kittens And Rabbits

Puppies

Puppies are nice
Puppies are fast
Puppies are cute
Puppies are hopeful
Puppies are good
Puppies aren't fierce
Puppies don't fight, they play.

Kittens

Kittens like playing
Kittens like scratching my back and hand
Kittens are hopeful
Kittens are cute
Kittens like fish
Kittens like chasing mice
Kittens are good.

Rabbits

Rabbits poo in your hand.

Autumn Mayers (7)
All Saints CE Primary School, Fulham

A Ball So Small

What can I do with a ball so small?
It's no good for kicking or flicking.
But it is good for sending in the mail
To my cousin, in Australia.
I can see him having a think,
A wink and a twinkle in his eye.
He'll come up with an idea for my small ball.
'It's not a ball mate, it's a marble!'
So that's what I did with my small ball.

Oscar Bell (8)
All Saints CE Primary School, Fulham

The Ancient Rumpus

The ancient Egyptians
Loved their inscriptions
They did them all day long
The people who wrote them
Were intelligent scribes
And were often found eating pear pies, pear pies
And were often found eating pear pies.

The ancient Greeks
Loved their seats
They sat down all day long
The people who made them
Were boys and girls
And were often found playing with pearls, with pearls
And were often found playing with pearls.

The ancient Romans
Loved their poems
They read them all day long
The people who bought them
Were funny and cool
And were often found taming a bull, a bull
And were often found taming a bull.

Bridie Barton (7)
All Saints CE Primary School, Fulham

The Animal Rap

Have you seen the porcupine's spikes?
They will give you midnight frights.
Have you heard the cat miaow?
That's his way of saying, 'Ow!'
Have you seen the elephant's trunk?
You need to run and hide in your bunk.
Have you heard the tiger roar?
As he ran through the door.

Kyle Medler (9)
All Saints CE Primary School, Fulham

Autumn's Atmosphere

Crusty leaves
Falling, crunching, dying
Loves to feel the wispy air
Stirring.

Eva Paul (10)
All Saints CE Primary School, Fulham

Autumn's Meadows - Haiku

As the leaves fall down,
The stream runs by the meadows
And the leaves turn brown.

Beatrice Ker (10)
All Saints CE Primary School, Fulham

Trees

Growing, creating, poking
Making air of creatures
Important.

Ben Price (10)
All Saints CE Primary School, Fulham

Autumn - Haiku

Golden falling leaves,
Twirling, swirling through the air
Landing without care.

Tion Dennis (10)
All Saints CE Primary School, Fulham

Autumn - Haiku

Autumn is coming
The wind is blowing coldly,
Leaves are falling down.

Ruben Martin (11)
All Saints CE Primary School, Fulham

Beautiful Leaves

Colourful, star-like shape
Blowing, moving, falling
Loves to blow around in the air all day long
Marvellous.

Tijana Todorinovic (10)
All Saints CE Primary School, Fulham

Russets - Haiku

A golden apple,
Stuck in an old browning tree
Next day on the floor.

Amar Azaouzi (10)
All Saints CE Primary School, Fulham

Autumn - Haiku

Windy autumn days
When kids jump in golden leaves,
On the ground they lie.

Emma Sennett (10)
All Saints CE Primary School, Fulham

Beano

There was a young girl called Tasha,
Whose favourites were Dennis and Gnasher,
She read them all week,
Till her mum got the freaks,
Now all she can do is eat pasta!

Natasha Colebrook (8)
All Saints CE Primary School, Fulham

Autumn Leaves

Leaves
Gold and red
Falling, browning
Autumn is when leaves are flying
Windy.

Faisal Urfali (11)
All Saints CE Primary School, Fulham

My Poetry

Fulham are great, no team is better
If there is a better team
It would not exist!

I support them!

Emma Cowan (8)
All Saints CE Primary School, Fulham

Autumn - Haiku

Autumn is chilly
The trees are brown and frilly
Come and play today.

Mazie Reece (10)
All Saints CE Primary School, Fulham

Manchester United, Kings Of The Game

Manchester United, kings of the game
Football will never be the same
Rooney and Ronaldo score a lot of goals
When I'm at Old Trafford I see Paul Scholes
Rooney's crazy, he's cuckoo, he's getting mad
Don't get sent off or we'll be sad
For Man United you're our star
Wayne Rooney will go far
Van Nistelrooy stands so proud
Then the crowd shouts so loud
He's going so fast down the wing
Come on Ruud, you're our king
Now what's happening? He's on the ground
Referee, you German hound!
But what's he saying? It's a penalty
Thank you, thank you, referee!
They score a goal by Van Nistelrooy!

James Fawkes (8)
All Saints CE Primary School, Fulham

Watch Out, Watch Out

Watch out, watch out, it's Hallowe'en
Hiding in the shadows, creeping round your house
Waiting to scare you.
When the night falls
And the ghosts call
To wizards and witches.
When it is 31st October, stay at home,
For this is when the monsters roam.

Watch out, watch out, it's Hallowe'en.

Alex Godfray (8)
All Saints CE Primary School, Fulham

About Our Name

My name is Anayah and what can I say,
I love it when my mum and dad call me Na Na.
So listen to my name and listen to it good
Anayah. I have a few nicknames like Na and Nay Nay
And those are my two favourite nicknames.
I think many people in Britain
Haven't got the same name as me.
I think my name is quite nice, it is not lame,
It is not plain and it contains six letters.
Don't let people laugh in your face
With shame about your name.
It doesn't matter about how many letters
Your name contains.
No matter how old you are,
Just as long as you love your special name.

Anayah George (9)
All Saints CE Primary School, Fulham

The Rest Of My Day

When I come home
My nan lets me play with a ball,
Then Tommy comes to play inside
We go in the garden and play on the slide.
Then on the swing we to and fro,
I ask Tommy in for tea,
So there is Nanny, Tommy and me.
Lemonade, sandwiches and cake galore,
We always want more and more.
Then it's time for Tommy to go,
Goodnight.

Robbie Rudge (8)
All Saints CE Primary School, Fulham

You Make Me Feel!

You make me feel like a cat!
You make me feel very fat!

You make me feel like a log!
You make me feel like a frog!

You make me feel very cold!
You make me feel very old!

You make me feel sad!
You make me feel very mad!

You make me feel like a pound of jelly!
You make me feel like Big Daddy's belly!

You make me feel like a car!
You make me go very far!

You make me feel like climbing the wall!
You make me feel like I'm going to fall!

You make me feel like a flower, lily!
You make me feel very silly!

Hannah Mercer (8)
All Saints CE Primary School, Fulham

Think Nature

I like gardening a lot.
I even have my own flower pot.
All the carrots are as colourful as a parrot.
All the mud on top of the bud.
The way to sow is to throw.
All the flowers have a power,
But seeds sometimes turn into weeds.
There are lots of leaves on all the trees.
All the green beans are so clean.
It's a wonderful scene.

Tilda Bates (8)
All Saints CE Primary School, Fulham

My Little Brother

When I was seven my brother was born,
The first thing he did was give a big yawn.

When we were in hospital we saw my mum
Holding my baby brother's little thumb.

When we got home later that day
We laid him in the crib, as they did with Jesus
On that special day

He woke for a bottle three times a night
And sometimes he gave me a little fright.

In the beginning he was boring and did nothing
Now he's always up to something.

We went to the park and had a laugh
He wore a little blue hat and a little blue scarf.

He's now saying, 'Dad' and 'Mummy' too
It won't be long till he's saying football tunes.

I love my brother, he loves me too
Apart from when he puts my school shoes down the *loo!*

Paige Coote (8)
All Saints CE Primary School, Fulham

Teachers

T eaching teachers teaching us!
E njoyable work with our fun teacher!
A ll our subjects are really fun!
C hildren enjoying every minute of school!
H appy children being taught!
E ducation is so much fun!
R unning fast in PE!
S itting silently surfing the web!

Luke Stilwell (8)
All Saints CE Primary School, Fulham

Tongue Twisters

I saw shells sold on the
sandy soft beach.
They smelt smelly but I
saw them sway.

Over my shoulder
I saw a silent soldier
standing straight. Silently,
I saw him with
other soldiers all
standing straight.

I went on a train trip, it
went tremendously
fast. I was too tired to
stay too long.

My teacher taught
me tonnes of things.
I see her talk and
teach, she is tall
and talks about
tons of fairy tales.

I travelled on a bus to go
on a boat to a big house.
There were big bees biting.

I have seen a
huge house with
humungous plants.
I heard them hum
hard and it smelt of honey.

Juliette Hannay (9)
All Saints CE Primary School, Fulham

Capital Experiences

When I was in Bern,
I met with Fern.
She made Gruyère cheese,
With such great ease.

While I was in Spain,
I had a great pain,
From what I did,
Playing football in Madrid.

In Cairo on a camel,
Which is a mammal,
I saw pyramids and the Nile.
A river 4,160 miles.

When I was in Rome,
I saw the Pope and some domes,
Lots of stray cats in the square,
And many churches everywhere.

If to Beijing I go,
The facts that I know,
One billion people there are,
And it is very far.

In Paris in Luxembourg Gardens,
With lots of excuses and pardons,
Cousin Luke and I rode our bikes,
And I met a new friend called Mike.

But London is my home,
Not Tallinn, Sofia or Rome,
It's a place that I hold dear,
Friends and family always near.

Nathaniel B Ballard (8)
All Saints CE Primary School, Fulham

Me And Doris

Me and Doris are a great team, we go everywhere together.

When we go to the park we run and play.
I throw her a ball, we could stay there all day.

Sometimes she's dirty so I give her a wash,
Doris doesn't like it because it makes her look posh.

Doris loves it when I tickle her tummy,
She lies on her back and finds it funny.

When she sits I give her a treat,
It's only a biscuit as she doesn't have meat.

Sometimes she's naughty and chases the cat,
Fergie runs away as she doesn't like that.

Me and Doris are a great team, we do everything together.

I love Doris and she loves me.

Georgina Connolly (8)
All Saints CE Primary School, Fulham

All About Fireworks

The 5th of November
Is a day to remember
Bonfires burning bright
It's such a beautiful sight
Standing by the sparkly light
Rockets flying in the sky
Big loud bangs make babies cry
Cats and dogs kept away
Tomorrow they can go out to play
Catherine wheels that spin round and round
Jumping Jacks and bangers on the ground
Fireworks here, sparklers there
It's all great fun but we must take care
Oh what a fantastic day because it's also my
birthday.

Georgia Connor (8)
All Saints CE Primary School, Fulham

Autumn

A utumn leaves go brown, red and yellow
U nder the trees all around
T rees go bare, no more colour
U pon the ground
M any roots die
N o more flowers around.

Ashleigh Wyatt (8)
All Saints CE Primary School, Fulham

Autumn - Haiku

This autumn is damp,
Children are running to school,
Hallowe'en is near.

Amalia Nigl (10)
All Saints CE Primary School, Fulham

My Pet Rabbit

My rabbit has a habit
He chooses to chew my shoes
And not my sister's shoes.
He thinks my shoes taste of chewy chews.
My rabbit has a funny habit.

Salih Ergench (8)
All Saints CE Primary School, Fulham

Leaf Luck - Haiku

When the leaves all drop
You know luck is in the air
People catching leaves.

Matilda McNair (10)
All Saints CE Primary School, Fulham

Autumn

Squirrels
Rusty brown
Hopping and jumping
Up and down trees
Playful.

Danielle Walker (10)
All Saints CE Primary School, Fulham

Autumn - Haiku

The autumn is cold
It blows all the leaves like mad
While it gets colder.

Joseph Hartigan (10)
All Saints CE Primary School, Fulham

Autumn

Autumn
Cold, windy
Floating, moving, dancing
Loves to wind about,
Leaves.

Kane Aidoo-Williams (10)
All Saints CE Primary School, Fulham

Autumn - Haiku

The air is chilly
And all leaves have fallen down
The trees lose their hair.

Amy Shamsi (10)
All Saints CE Primary School, Fulham

Autumn Days - Haiku

Autumn is coming
Today, brown leaves are forming
All trees are swaying.

Milena Agbaba (10)
All Saints CE Primary School, Fulham

The Jungle

J ump into the jungle
U nder the trees,
N aughty monkeys swinging in the breeze.
G iraffes are eating leaves
L ike vegetarian thieves.
E veryone is happy, even the bees!

Ella Kennedy (7)
Bassett House School, Kensington

Football

It is a good sport, doing football.
You practise scoring goals.
You also practise passing the ball to each other.
Then when you go to a football match
You can win the game.

Kapriel Chiarini (7)
Bassett House School, Kensington

My Liberty

I was free, not in school
I would dance, play, skip and jump.
I would run about in the fields, laugh and sing.
The buttercups, the daisies, the roses, the poppies
That's how I would spend my day!

Isobel Barnard (7)
Bassett House School, Kensington

Mermaid

Mermaid, mermaid, mermaid splashing in the sea.
Green, blue and yellow tails for you and me.

Mermaid, mermaid, mermaid splashing in the sea,
Gold hair, silver and green, jump in the moonlight
Jumping in the sea.
The sea splashing against the rocks.

Phoebe Flatau (8)
Bassett House School, Kensington

Christmas Eve

Hot chocolate by the fire,
The presents underneath the tree.
Christmas bells ringing,
People singing Christmas carols.
Nice and warm in bed
But thinking of the poor
Sitting out there in the cold snow instead.
Singing carols is so jolly.

India Hall (7)
Bassett House School, Kensington

The Frog!

One day I saw a frog.
It went hop, hop, stop!
The frog went, 'Croak.'
And then got soaked!
I love frogs I hope you do.
I've never seen a frog poo!

Holly Sommers (7)
Bassett House School, Kensington

Thank You

Thank you for . . .
The smell of the soft smoke coming from
A glittering firework shimmering in the night sky,
The feel of a prickly holly, poking against my skin,
The touch of a cold white snowball falling from a mountain.

Thank you for . . .
The sound of a robin chirping, at Christmas in the morning,
The view of a sunset settling down
With orange and red in the background,
The waves bashing against the rocks.

Thank you for . . .
The pink rose cheeks on a cat's face,
The gold hard glistening coins from a treasure chest,
The swirly colourful rainbow sparkling in the sky.

Lily Cullinane (9)
Bassett House School, Kensington

Thank You

Thank you for . . .
the crackling fireworks at night glistening to the ground,
a feeling of a thorn prickling against your skin.

Thank you for . . .
the taste of all the different food, sizzling on your tongue,
a taste you might never forget.

Thank you for . . .
the sound of laughter and happiness
filling you with joy,
a memory that will stay in your head.

Milen Ghebremichael (9)
Bassett House School, Kensington

Thank You

Thank you for . . .
the rushing sapphire Indian sea,
the twinkling stars in the dusty black sky,
the smell of nature filling my body.

Thank you for . . .
the kindness of my smiling friends,
the touch of my fluffy guinea pigs,
the memories of places my family have taken me to.

Thank you for . . .
the music from the howling wind,
the silhouette of an icy mountain,
the opening of exciting places.

Elsa Perryman-Owens (9)
Bassett House School, Kensington

Lonely House

(This poem is dedicated to an abandoned house
on Bramley Road on the way to school)

Poor house, oh poor house,
You look like a poor old lady
Alone on the street,
I want to give you company, a friend.

Poor house, oh poor house,
You look like a poor animal
Locked in a cage.
I want to give you freedom
And make you happy.

You will never be alone again,
I promise.

Chiara Baldini (8)
Bassett House School, Kensington

Thank You

Thank you for . . .
the feel of warm velvet chocolate, melting in my mouth,
soft feathers against my cheek,
my joyful smiling kittens, curled up on my bed.

Thank you for . . .
the crunching of snow under my feet,
the crackling excitement of opening a present,
the fresh crispy food, that we gobble down each day.

Thank you for . . .
the glistening fountains cascading with water,
the gigantic mountains we climb and discover,
the cuddly cotton we wear to keep us warm.

Susannah Slevin (9)
Bassett House School, Kensington

Katy The Poem

Katy is a very cute little sister.
She likes wearing a pink dress every day.
She has greeny-blue eyes and shouts
And screams a lot.
She is very nice when she is nice
And horrid when she is horrid!
She doesn't eat very much things like pasta.
Her favourite food is chicken nuggets.
She hates any type of pasta.
Her favourite fruit is apple,
Her favourite veg is carrot.
Lucy's poem, Lucy's poem, Lucy's poem.

Lucy Hanson (7)
Bassett House School, Kensington

Thank You

Thank you for . . .
The taste of melting chocolate falling gently into my mouth.
The glittering fireworks shooting past the stars.
The cries of a tumbling mountain.

Thank you for . . .
The melody of an early bird calling my name.
The memory of my angel's angelic attitude.
The flame of the sizzling sun, burning my finger.

Thank you for . .
The smell of purple fumes snaking up my nose.
The multicoloured sight of a setting sunset,
Falling soundlessly under the ground.

Thank you for . . .
The roaring night of the storm's first rush.
The crackling crimson fire fizzing selfishly.
The raging river with the sapphire glisten.

Holly Hirsch (9)
Bassett House School, Kensington

Dark Rider

Dark rider rides through the trees,
With his sword up to his knees.
His dark cloak waves in the breeze
And the little wood fairies nearly start to *freeze!*

Dark rider whips his horse
And the old oak nearly falls!
Little mice scramble into holes
While young foxes feast on moles.

Arianna Vince (8)
Bassett House School, Kensington

Flowers

Flowers are the prettiest, flowers are beautiful,
Flowers have the nicest smell,
They have pretty colours like pink and blue.
Flowers are the most exciting,
So flowers are the best.
You smell the flowers
When you're running down the stream
And you see them in fields.
Sometimes there's a whole field of them
Lots of times I smell a beautiful smell
And if I'm lucky I sometimes
See the great poppies which are beautiful.
I just wish I had a garden of flowers.

Hannah Sidwell (7)
Bassett House School, Kensington

Sandy

My horse has a lovely sandy back,
her mane and tail are white,
and she shimmers in the moonlight.

She eats carrots and apples
and cackles out a neigh,
she also sleeps on soft smooth hay.

Her stable is made of oak wood
and she never ever chokes.

She's the best horse in the world.

Sophie Stretch (7)
Bassett House School, Kensington

Mr Chill's Bucket

Mr Chill had a bucket,
Which he never ever lent,
For fear it might receive a dent.
Then again you could never tell,
Thought Mr Chill, some fool might
Chuck it down the well.
When the news spread
That Mr Chill was dead,
All the people in the village said,
'He's sure gone with his bucket to Hell.'
What a surprise it was to find,
Mr Chill's bucket full of coins inside,
And a little note that read,
'This is to buy a new church bell'.

Kwarteng Opoku Sarfo (9)
Coleraine Park Primary School, Tottenham

The Bird Of Birds

I am the bird of birds - I fly
The everlasting bird!
I flew over the sky,
The everlasting bird!
I built a lovely nest,
The everlasting bird!
I think I'm the best,
The everlasting bird!
I eat my meat,
The everlasting bird!
I had a cosy seat,
The everlasting bird!

Marcus Brown (9)
Coleraine Park Primary School, Tottenham

Global Warming

Our planet is in a bad condition and very sick
    Why are people polluting it?
        Are they thick?

Throwing rubbish, creating litter
    Making our roads seem bitter
        It just isn't fair
            Don't you care?

The ice poles are melting, creating a big flood
    People drown, suffer and die
        What a waste of blood
            Why pollute the air
                Don't you care?

Using cars increase the pollution
    Walking is the solution.

So please if you could
    Reduce the pollution for your own good.

Angelo Reinoso (9)
Coleraine Park Primary School, Tottenham

My Simpsons' Poem

The person who always tidies up for them,
Is the mum of the house, who is Marge.
She cooks, cleans and loves them but her hair is very large.
The troublemaker of the house is the son whose name is Bart,
Whilst his father Homer only drinks, burps and farts.
Maggie is one and she cannot yet speak.
Lisa is smart, that's why people class her as a geek.
Homer's arch-enemy is a Christian called Ned
Who makes Homer angry to make his face go red.

Tyrell Locker-Mcgrowder (10)
Coleraine Park Primary School, Tottenham

The Weather

The weather is sweet
The weather is dry
The weather is hot like a blueberry pie.

The weather is wet
The weather is cloudy
The weather and sky look very lousy.

The sun shines like the brightest star
The sun is bright and colourful
The sun sings loudly la-de-da.

The rain drizzles and pelts
The rain hits you then melts.

The wind blows you away
The wind really is fast
They said it was windy on the weather forecast.

Anelsie Burlingham
Coleraine Park Primary School, Tottenham

Basketball

Now basketball is my favourite sport,
I like it when I dribble it up and down the court,
I keep it so fresh on the microphone,
There is no interception on the game zone,
I like slam dunk,
Giggle with the punk,
So there,
So there,
Basketball is my mate,
I hold the cup every time that's great,
Go basketball.

Youcef Ouaar (9)
Coleraine Park Primary School, Tottenham

The Bird Of Birds

I am the bird of birds - I fly
The everlasting bird,
I fly around the sky so sly
The everlasting bird
I go on my golden quest
The everlasting bird
My golden quest is to build a nest
The everlasting bird
I drink my water from the river
The everlasting bird
And on very cold nights I shiver and shiver
The everlasting bird
I eat my seeds, I eat and eat
The everlasting bird
Then I go outside and feel the heat
The everlasting bird
I see a robin redbreast
The everlasting bird
I say to it I'm the best
The everlasting bird.

Ryan White (9)
Coleraine Park Primary School, Tottenham

The Cat Of Cats

I am the cat of cats
    the everlasting cat

I am old and as sleek as jam
    the everlasting cat

I hunt vermin in the night
    the everlasting cat

For I see best without light
    the everlasting cat.

Shannon-Louise Geoghegan (9)
Coleraine Park Primary School, Tottenham

Hula Hoop Heaven

Round and round
Round again
With rhythm
Style and energy
Until you start to slow down
And then it will drop on the ground
Pick it up and start again
Then we start again
Then the fun begins again
Pink, blue, yellow, green
Time we start to feel the best
We can twist, twirl day and night,
Keep on going until the fight.

Joy Princess Gardiner (9)
Coleraine Park Primary School, Tottenham

School

You go to school to learn,
It gives you education,
It's where you get good marks
If you have dedication.

It could be fun,
It could be boring,
But it doesn't matter
Because you're learning.

School is fun,
School is great,
School is the best thing
So don't be late.

Tashana Nelson (9)
Coleraine Park Primary School, Tottenham

Teachers

T eachers are the best
E ven at a test
A teacher wants you to be nice
C hat, chat, chat is not good that's why she says it twice
H owever you listen to your teacher she would be glad
E ven sometimes she can be sad
R udeness is bad that's what the teacher says
S ometimes when she feels happy, she joins us and plays.

Mine Kizilkaya (9)
Coleraine Park Primary School, Tottenham

Clapping

Clap to the rhythm,
Clap to the beat,
Clap to the song,
And tell me it's sweet
Use your powerful energy
So you could make it interesting
You could do it on time
If you want to be mine.

Mihriban Kinik & Rodi Kurt (9)
Coleraine Park Primary School, Tottenham

Playground Fun

You run you jump
You spring
You jog you hop you skip
Playing merrily with your friends
Playground fun just never ends.

Corey Powell-Strachan & Nada Loudiyi (8)
Coleraine Park Primary School, Tottenham

Basketball Fun

I scored
A goal,
I feel so very great.
The ball is bouncing up and down.
Quickly running faster, faster.
I'm giggling with lots of laughter.
Shouting and moving with a basketball.
Running and playing in the playground.
Memories, memories grooving around.

Shane-Curtis Hines (8)
Coleraine Park Primary School, Tottenham

Jesse Owens

Jesse is a cheetah jumping on his prey.
He is like a car racing through the day.
His feet are bowling balls rolling round tracks.
His legs are like springs or a jumping Jack.
He is a *world champ* hip hip hooray.
He has gold medals like Kelly Holmes,
What more can I say.

Melissa Roberts (10)
Coleraine Park Primary School, Tottenham

Basketball

I'm like Michael Jordan
Always trying to score.
In the playground bouncing the ball.
Passing the ball to my friends,
Just before my basketball dream ends.

Georja Matthew & Ella Stephen-Oladele (8)
Coleraine Park Primary School, Tottenham

High And Low

Jump, jump, jump
As high as you can.
Be careful though
I might jump on your hand.
Jump high, jump low
Jump as much as you can
Have energy,
Have fun
Have as much as you can.

Afua Agyeman (8)
Coleraine Park Primary School, Tottenham

Skipping

We skip with energy
Big and strong
You can skip with us, come along.
Lorita and Helin the best girls,
We are very good at doing the twirls.
Round and round we twirl and twirl.
We fall down and start to whirl.

Lorita Abazi & Helin Dogan (8)
Coleraine Park Primary School, Tottenham

Jesse Owens

Jesse Owens is as hot as the sun,
He is as cool as sunglasses,
He is like lightning giving a shock,
He is as sharp as a pencil,
He is like a mower taking out the grass,
He is like a friend always helping.

Demi Spencer (10)
Coleraine Park Primary School, Tottenham

High And Low

High and low
Jump, jump, jump
As high as you can.
Be careful though
I might jump on your hand
Jump high, jump low
Jump as much as you can.
Have energy
Have fun
Have as much as you can.

Afua Agyeman & Lateschar Tyrell (8)
Coleraine Park Primary School, Tottenham

Jumping Fun

Jumping fast,
Jumping slow,
Jumping is fun,
As we go.

Jumping with strength,
Jumping with power,
Jumping with joy
And for one hour.

Jennifer De Oliveria & Savannah (8)
Coleraine Park Primary School, Tottenham

It's My Job

It's my job to clean my room
My mum's job is to wash the spoons
My dad's job is to wash the car
My brother's job is to clean the garage.

Haleema Nazir (7)
Gordonbrock Primary School, Brockley

Going In The Restaurant

Sit
down at the table
Order
the delicious food
Munch
the barbecue chicken and chips
Have
a food fight
The baby turns green
throws
up all over my new dress
Yuck!
It's green!
I
hate vomit and Mum is not angry.
So
I get a fist full of chips
Aim! Fire! Bullseye! *Waa!* Mum
is angry!

Jessica Eschoe-Naylor (8)
Gordonbrock Primary School, Brockley

It's My Job . . .

It's my job
to keep my room tidy
It's Mum's job
to cook the dinner,
squashy tomatoes
It's my job
to wake my lazy brother
It's my job
to eat the food.

Maia Okoloba (7)
Gordonbrock Primary School, Brockley

Yum Yum, Dinner Time

It's my job
To lay the table
It's Mum's job
To roast the golden brown chicken
It's my job
To call my lazy sister
It's Mum's job
To cook the wonderful spaghetti
It's my job
To eat the golden brown chicken
With the wonderful spaghetti
Mmm finished.

Rhiannon Miller-Douglas (8)
Gordonbrock Primary School, Brockley

It's My Job

It's my job
to lay the table
It's Mum's job
to peel the potatoes
It's my job
to make the cake
It's Mum's job
to put the cake in the oven
It's my job
to lick the bowl clean
It's Mum's job
to save the cake
It's my job
to eat the cake
It's my job
to wash the plates.

Moya Biggs Teiona (9)
Gordonbrock Primary School, Brockley

Oh Spaghetti

Spaghetti, spaghetti
So curly and hot
So squidgy with some sauce
Mmm . . .

Spaghetti, spaghetti
I can't get enough
Spaghetti, spaghetti
I love you a lot.

Oh spaghetti you're so sticky
And squishy and covered with sauce
Delicious and hot
You burn my tongue
Ouch!

Oh spaghetti.

Layla Saleemi (8)
Gordonbrock Primary School, Brockley

Honey, Honey

Honey, honey
You are so yummy
Sit in my tummy
Mummy, Mummy
Can I have some honey?

Honey, honey
It is lovely
It's yummny
I want more honey, Mummy!

I've had enough honey
Not so yummy!

Hazel Dawson (8)
Gordonbrock Primary School, Brockley

It's My Job

Munch
My crunchy cherries
Crunch
My chocolaty Coco Pops
Chop
My bendy banana
Lick
My little lollipop.

Anisa Mohammed (8)
Gordonbrock Primary School, Brockley

It's My Job

It's my job to lay the table
It's Mum's job to cook the chicken
It's my job to wash my hands
It's Mum's job to put the chicken in the oven
It's my job to gobble it up
It's Mum's job to get the pudding
It's my job to wash up.

Mignone Aina (8)
Gordonbrock Primary School, Brockley

Food - Haiku

Yummy ice cream *mmm* . . .
Chocolate cake my favourite
Eat too much get ill.

Hawa Ali (7)
Gordonbrock Primary School, Brockley

Hot Chocolate Cake

It is so spongy and soft
I secretly eat you in the loft
Hot chocolate cake
I love you so much
Even the Dutch
Love chocolate so much!
Lovely lemon not for me
Cheesecake full of variety
Squash, squish, squelch in my mouth
So lovely it makes me belch!
Sometimes I even put on hot chocolate sauce
I'd have it in a food course
I love you so much
Chocolate cake
You're my mate!

Lauren Harris (9)
Gordonbrock Primary School, Brockley

Roman Days Food - Gerbils

Gerbils are delicious
Gerbils are great
Gerbils are rodents
I don't hate

Gerbils are creamy
Gerbils are grey
I'm going to eat one today.
Gerbils
Mmm . . .
Slurp finished!

Kwadwo Kankam (8)
Gordonbrock Primary School, Brockley

Waiting For Ribs

Sit on the sofa
With my brother
Waiting
Waiting
Waiting
And
Waiting for my dinner.

Mum in the kitchen
On her own
Cooking
Cooking
Cooking
Cooking my ribs.
Finally they're ready
My mum says,
'Come and get your ribs,'
So I run
to the kitchen and
get my ribs
and take
them to the table
and chew, chew, chew, my spicy ribs
yum!

Zachary Alamir Quallo (8)
Gordonbrock Primary School, Brockley

Strawberries

Strawberries, strawberries
Sweet and juicy
Yum yum in my tum
They taste good
Yummy, scrummy
In my tummy.

Amber Lawrence (8)
Gordonbrock Primary School, Brockley

Spaghetti

Slimy slurpy spaghetti
Yummy, yummy in my tummy
Slurpy spaghetti, it is really in my tummy
Peas no please
Please, oh thank you Dad
Dinner time, dinner time
Not again, alright then
I am going to eat slowly
What is for dinner? Peas *yuck!*
What kind of peas? Mushed up peas
Yuck! Yuck! Yuck it goes in my mouth
It is hot, hot, hot
Mum make spaghetti
Which is slimy, slippery
Delicious and wriggly
Spaghetti is really yummy
I put it into my mouth
It is wriggly
What you know spaghetti
Slurpy, slurpy in my tummy
It is really in my tummy.

Fatih Gök (8)
Gordonbrock Primary School, Brockley

Pancakes

Pancakes with syrup on top,
Dripping and dropping with everything it's got,
Precious pancake, pretty pancake, powerful pancake,
You're delicious, you're fantastic,
Sweet syrup on a pancake, it's dripping on my face,
Floppy pancake, floppy pancake,
You're magnificent, spectacular, you're so tasty.
Every morning I'll have you, I love you,
Powerful, precious, pretty, ploppy pancake, I love you.

Ceykan Ramadan (9)
Gordonbrock Primary School, Brockley

Sit Down At The Table

Sit down at the table
Stop laughing
When you eat
Noodles are swirly
And nice
I hate it with
Tomato also
With cucumber
Some are swirly
Some are long
Some are wide
With the same pride
It tastes yummy
It sounds silent
Moves quickly
Also it's nice
With some spice.

Dhilon Selvaratnam (8)
Gordonbrock Primary School, Brockley

Untitled

I was waiting for my dinner,
Stomping for my dinner.
I want my curry now,
I don't like my curry.
Mum I want dessert now instead.
It was yum-yum.
It was nice.
I want to go to bed.
No it is too early.
I'm hungry.
I want it now Mum.

Ronnie Tharme
Gordonbrock Primary School, Brockley

Sausages

I love sausage sandwiches,
Sausages sizzling in a pan.
I bite them, swallow them,
I crunch them, I munch them.
I cry, 'Mum, Mum,
In my tummy
I love this Mummy.'
I swallow them again,
I just crunch them,
I say to my mummy,
'There is rumbling in my tummy.'
This is lovely Mummy,
I just can't get enough!

Megan Gosnell (8)
Gordonbrock Primary School, Brockley

My Food Poem

Slurpy spaghetti
Cooking in the hot
Sizzling pan,
It is yum, yum, yum
In my tum.
The slurpy spaghetti
Slithers down my tum, tum,
Like a small worm crawling
Down into my mouth,
I crunch it, munch it, again.

Zekiye Hamit (9)
Gordonbrock Primary School, Brockley

I Love Noodles

Noodles, lovely
Noodles, it's slurpy
They look like
Worms underground
When is it ready
I love it.

Chicken I love it

The chicken
Popping, popping in the pan
The spinning fan
A blowing air
And my hair is blowing in the air
The chicken
I love it, smell it in the air.

Benjamin White (8)
Gordonbrock Primary School, Brockley

Chips

They're hot and long.
They're salty and yummy.
All covered in ketchup and sprinkled with vinegar.
They sizzle in the oven, before they wriggle down my throat.
I'll blow to make the hot ones go,
They will go all warm.
I will bite one end off.
I'll blow so it's yummy,
And it will wriggle down my tummy.
I love chips!

Milo Harper (8)
Gordonbrock Primary School, Brockley

Chocolate Cake And Custard

Chocolate cake and custard
You're so soft and squidgy
Slimy and grimy
As it melts in the sauce
It makes me warm and cosy and super great
Oh hot custard and chocolate cake
I would have more for breakfast if I could
Sometimes I have it with whipped cream.
Chocolate cake oh chocolate cake
You'll always be my best mate.

Georgia South (8)
Gordonbrock Primary School, Brockley

Perfect Pizza

Munch, crunch the crust
I love you I do
I love you.
Dripping down my T-shirt.
Tomato, pepperoni
Hot or cold you're perfect
I love you, I do.
Margerita, pepperoni,
I love you, I do.
Spicy, hot, normal or freezing
I love you.
Pizza, pizza
Yum, yum, yum!
Slice it in half,
Slice it in quarters
Peas is for tea
Not peas, pizza
Yum, yum, yum!

Ella Elizabeth Puttick (8)
Gordonbrock Primary School, Brockley

Juicy, Juicy, Mango

Monkey mango
Down my throat
Gobble, gobble
Slurp, slurp
My mouth wants to water
When my teeth are grinding through
Can't you hear that squashy noise
Yum-yum in my tum
Mangoes are so essential
My mouth is dripping with mango juice
Really, really juicy!

Jasmin Winifred (8)
Gordonbrock Primary School, Brockley

Perfect Pizza

Pizza, pizza
You're perfect
Hot
Cold
Warm
Your tomato sauce dripping
Down
Me!
Margerita with ham
It's my favourite!
Pizza, pizza
You're the best!

Siân Ella Keogh (8)
Gordonbrock Primary School, Brockley

Hilarious Hot Dogs

Heating hot dogs,
ready
to
eat.
Stuff in the mouth,
blow
hot
blow.
Running round the room,
blowing
out
smoke.
Finally down the throat,
one hot time,
never to forget.
Have another one,
but
happens
once
again!

Isabelle Charlotte Webb (8)
Gordonbrock Primary School, Brockley

My Food Poem

My food is ravishing,
It's lovely and hot,
It melts in my tum,
Oh it is yum.
I've got a butler,
His name is Steve,
He makes a marvellous feast.
So please Madam have some food,
Oh please.

Melissa Cunningham (8)
Gordonbrock Primary School, Brockley

Food

Lollipop

Pop pop, pop, lollipop,
Lauren lemony pop,
Loves lollipops.

Tomatoes

Timmy Tunic loves
Toxic tickly tomatoes,
Squish, squash, squish

Noodles

Nicky Noo loves
Knocky, knotty,
Noodles in her,
Tummy, yummy, yummy

Cucumbers

Clarice Clan
Loves cutie,
Cool cucumbers
Because they're
Crunchy and cunning.

India Chetta-Roberts (9)
Gordonbrock Primary School, Brockley

Noodles

Come on EJ
Come on EJ
Dinner is on your plate . . .
Noodles, noodles, noodles . . .
On this very plate
Mmm yum-yum
In this very tum you go.

Ethan Vella (8)
Gordonbrock Primary School, Brockley

Munch

My crunchy Cheerios
Crunch
My chocolaty Coco Pops
Chop
My bendy banana
Lick
My little lollipop.

Alfie Hoy (7)
Gordonbrock Primary School, Brockley

The Depressed Football

I am
Round, hard, depressed
Because of little children
Booting me across the playground
Like I'm nothing
My skin is tearing
All because of you

Why
Do you kick me so hard?
My skin is breaking
It hurts
All because of you

I want
You to stop kicking me
Like a punch bag
My heart is tearing
I want to rest
In peace.

Khalid Meeajun (10)
Holy Trinity Primary School, Maresfield Gardens

The Helpless Bush

I am frustrated with people shifting me about
Like an uneaten Brussels sprout
I am restless from hearing children cowardly shout
Like a fisherman that sells rotten old trout

I am practically destroyed that no one cares for me
And when they have to they just flee
The caretaker is obviously scatterbrained
If I meet him I think I just might faint

I especially like the three-year-olds
They treat my leaves like special gold
The Year 6s, oh don't say a word
The things they do are just absurd

Adults beat me like a phoney tree
While their babies disobey me
Is it because I'm not large
That I can't be in charge?

I am the helpless bush
Don't tell me to shush
Don't give me a push
Or I'll turn to mush

I am frustrated with people shifting me about
Like an uneaten Brussels sprout
I am restless from children that cowardly shout
Like a fisherman that sells rotten old trout.

Iman Abdulrahman (10)
Holy Trinity Primary School, Maresfield Gardens

The Depressed Hula Hoop

I go round and round
until I drop onto the ground
like stones being thrown into the sea.

I get picked up and thrown by other nasty children,
my other helpful friends are different colours,
they have the same life as me!

I like my colour, my colour is blue,
I am made of worn-out plastic
and when I go round it's like the world is spinning like a spinning top,
I feel dizzy
You viciously hit me on the ground,
I can feel the vibrations slicing me like a knife.

I work so hard to try and make people happy,
by winning or making them joyful
while playing with those little children.
My head gets squeezed by your cold hands.
Do you really care for me?

Zara Preston (10)
Holy Trinity Primary School, Maresfield Gardens

The Injured Basketball

I am
Bouncy,
I am full of energy but that doesn't mean you can fall on me or
Throw me around,
Or bounce me.

You can't
Throw me on the plants, some plants are spiky and pointy like
A knife.
I don't like that,
I don't like the smell of them, they stink like dogs
I don't like their green leaves,
I don't like bright green but I do like orange.

I know
You don't wash your hands
When you go to the toilet
Is that why you throw me around in other filthy hands?

Thank you
Girls at least you wash your hands, but why do you
Throw me around?
I thought you were softies
But you're tougher than the boys.

Atousa Faraji Khyabani (10)
Holy Trinity Primary School, Maresfield Gardens

The Frustrated Fountain

I've had
Enough of you!
Pulling my beautiful gleaming leg
It hurts you know!

I don't
Like it when you
Suck out my insides
It doesn't feel pleasant.

How would
You like it if
I sucked out your insides,
You wouldn't like it so don't do it to me!

You make
Me furious!
Every time you drink
From me I get
Hot and bothered,
Because of your breath.
I don't enjoy smelling it.
It doesn't smell wonderfully
Minty at all!
There, I think I've made my point.

Jasmine Crossey (10)
Holy Trinity Primary School, Maresfield Gardens

The Frustrated Water Fountain

I am
Irritated, tired and stressed because of you.
I am annoyed by your grim, stiff hands
Touching my rusty button for some of my cold, fresh water.

I've had enough of you
Throwing dark, hard rocky stones at me,
Then my cracks start to bleed with drips of pure clean water.
I've had enough of you
Wasting my bubbling, sweet water
By spitting it on the cool, concrete ground.

I can't
Stand you anymore, you in a queue unsteady
Pushing my silver button like a crazy donkey; *ee-aw!*
Not letting me breathe by keeping on pressing me.
I can't stand you anymore bashing your muddy football into me,
While the boiling, golden sun is reflecting on my folding white colour.

I know
Your dark secrets.
You hissing while sipping cool water in your big, chubby mouth.
I always hear you whispering your secrets.
Now I know what you have stole from the teacher.

I wish
You could take care of me,
Taking cold water when you need it.
I wish you could treat me with pleasure
And gracefully
So I can gleam forever.
But now it's too late.
I am never going to twinkle and gleam.
What you are doing to me.
On the outside of me
It really is painful,
But it is also painful on the inside
Where my little frozen heart is.

Una Predanic (10)
Holy Trinity Primary School, Maresfield Gardens

The Dizzy Skipping Rope

I am
Irritated and annoyed,
I've had enough of your skipping.
Find something else to do,
Don't play with me,
Just leave me . . .
All alone!
I know
You don't want to hurt me,
But why do you do it?
Just leave me all alone, please.
I've had enough
Of you turning me around.
Every day I hate getting hurt.
Stop whipping me around.
I can't work anymore,
It's too hard.
I need to be all alone
Just by myself.
I'm exhausted.
I won't
Work harder
Just leave me *alone*.
I am the dizzy skipping rope.

Damjana Kevric (10)
Holy Trinity Primary School, Maresfield Gardens

The Gleaming Fountain

I am
Dazzling, glittering, shining in the sun,
Giving my water to everyone,
Watching how they drink it all,
When they're tired because of playing football.

I know
What flower you picked from the stem,
What scrummy chocolate you ate in front of me.
But I wouldn't dare tell of you,
Because you've been so great to me.

I've had
A glimpse of the pound you washed,
With my pure water then dried with a leaf,
Looking at it desperately, greedily,
Like you're looking at a chocolate cake.

I can't
Imagine me here without you.
You make me feel so famous,
But I know that when you grow up,
I'll stand here all alone,
Like a puddle in the desert.

I want
To always have friends,
Never be alone.
Be spotlessly clean all day.
But I know that you've grown up and left me
And that I'll never gleam again.

Sara Bianca Semic (10)
Holy Trinity Primary School, Maresfield Gardens

The Battered Goalpost

I am
Completely battered because of you,
I can't go to hospital because I'm stuck to the ground.
You're supposed to hit the net,
Not me too.

I know
The score so there's no point in cheating.
If you start an argument,
I wish I could do the beating.

I've had
Enough of your comet-like balls
Smashing like a whipping cane into my head.
Plus you do it every day
So the pain hurts so much
I can't get to bed.

I can't
Let you throw steel-hard balls at me,
Do painful karate moves on me
And most of all climb on me.

I want
To leave this rough playground.
I want to live in a real glittering basketball stadium,
Where I get treated like a king
And all the players know what they're doing.
I want to go now!

Laurie Wedderburn   (10)
Holy Trinity Primary School, Maresfield Gardens

The Annoyed Basketball

I am,
An annoyed, grumpy basketball
Being bounced all over the place
Grubby hands always snatching at me
And making me all grey like mud.

I know,
What you did to the boy
Who tried to hold me gently
You snatched me off him viciously
Which really hurt me actually.

I've had,
Enough of your horrible shouting
And arguing over me
Because it really hurts my poor lovely ears
That you can't see.

I can't
Handle you shooting me
Into the net
Because it rubs onto my face
And the net always argues with me, you see
It says, 'Ow don't hit me.'

I want
To have a fabulous life
Full of joy and happiness
Like a fountain who serves children one by one
Or a skipping rope that makes children laugh.
Why can't I just be one of them!

Gulten Geneci (10)
Holy Trinity Primary School, Maresfield Gardens

Beaten Up Basketball

I am
Irritated, being bounced in trees as tall as lamp posts;
Upset, being stung by bees;
Annoyed, getting bashed against the metal fence;
Afraid of flying like a rocket through the sky.

I know
Who threw my smaller brothers and sisters over the fence,
Who wiped their grimy grubby hands on me,
Who hid the soft balls somewhere out there,
Who messed up the plants and pretty flowers.

I've had
Enough of flying through the air
Without a parachute or safety net,
Being argued and yelled over
By noisy hazardous schoolchildren.

I can't
Let you chuck me over the fence,
Claw apart my delicate orange rubber skin,
Lob me through the air like I'm a useless paper plane,
Chuck me against the foul bin.

I want
To be used properly
By professional basketball players,
To be looked after and cared for
By someone who really cares.

Akira Leyow (10)
Holy Trinity Primary School, Maresfield Gardens

The Grief-Stricken Football

I am,
Exhausted and annoyed
You're always kicking me around
It hurts!
Your grubby boots are always smothering me.

I know,
You don't want to hurt me.
But can you go easy,
It feels like my brain vibrating.

I know,
You don't want to hurt me.
But can you go easy.

I've had,
Enough of you kicking me around
It's got to stop!
Your feet should be as soft as cotton
And fluffy as candyfloss.

I won't
Accept it,
Please don't put your full power on me.
I am really like a cuddly teddy bear,
Not like a wasp.
So don't put your full power on me.

Codie Dolcy-Grant (10)
Holy Trinity Primary School, Maresfield Gardens

The Depressed Skipping Rope

I am
A ropy snake turning, turning all the time.
I am decrepit
I am worn-out from getting whipped on the floor like
A slave being whipped in ancient Roman times by you.
I am more depressed than you or anyone could imagine.

I know
You need to do exercise
But don't use me
Use 'Jack the football' not me.
I know what you need, exercise
But don't use me.
I know what you need but you don't know what I need.

I've had enough
Of your talking, your gossiping
And of your secrets
I've had enough of your whipping me to the ground.

I can't
Let you treat me like a slave
I should
Treat you like that
I can't let you move me around like
Furniture in a house.

I want
To leave this playground
I want to rest in peace
I want to be gone from you
I want to go home
I want to rest in peace.

Sarhang Shafiq (10)
Holy Trinity Primary School, Maresfield Gardens

The Hopeless Plant

I'm so annoyed at you.
Whipping me with that hard ball
It feels like a sharp knife
Ripping me apart.

Oi you. Stop playing with my leaves.
Can't you hear me.
Oh my leaves.
Stop plucking. They are not hairy eyebrows.
The noise you make.
It sounds like a herd of elephants.

I'm hopeless.
You're so lucky.
If I was a lively human
I would bite your hair off.

Ah that would be paradise
And please stop plaiting my leaves
I'm really getting fed up with you.
Honestly.

Please! Stop annoying me.
Thank you for listening.
Goodbye.

Suzana Rracaj (10)
Holy Trinity Primary School, Maresfield Gardens

The Poor Marbles

I am
Always furious, exhausted.
Smelly like rotten eggs because of you
You never wash your hands while
You're eating, that's why I smell.
Then you throw me on purpose
Across the playground as quick as
A cheetah. After that you always
Hide me in the plants so no one can
Play with me and then you make
Little children cry like a rainy day.
Look how horrible you are to everyone.

I know
What you did, you quickly stole
Ten of my shiny marbles
As if they were yours
You went to the head teacher's office and stole
Four packs of head teacher's award stickers.
Then when you got home
You ate five chocolate eggs
Quietly without asking.

Dina Osman Ibrahim (10)
Holy Trinity Primary School, Maresfield Gardens

The Dizzy Skipping Rope

I am
A dizzy skipping rope
Dazed from hours of turning
Tired of being held by your hot sweaty hands
Battered after a lifetime of turning and being whipped on the ground
Like a leather whip on the side of a horse
Deaf as an old lady from your cheating

I know
All of your silly skipping games
Your tiresome teasing chants
The boys you like
The girls you hate
I know all that's in your tiny conceited souls
Of your spoilt bodies

I've had
Enough of you twirling me like a spinning top
Spying on me as if I'm a bit of mud
Shouting over my delicate complexion
Hitting me on the ground
So I'm as muddy as a football.

Madalena Leão (10)
Holy Trinity Primary School, Maresfield Gardens

The Furious Playground

I am old and cold because of you
Smelly because of you
Unhappy and worn-out because of you

I know
What you did to me
Littered me like I was the dustbin
Stamped on my head
And how you threw all the rubbish over the fence

I can't
Let your muddy shoes walk all over me
Like I'm the dirt
Your spit running down my face
And I just can't go on with it
Your heavy bodies like one big, giant rock

I've had
Enough of your silly arguments
Growling like one thousand lions
You stomp over me
I've had enough of you standing on me

I want
You to leave me alone
To clean up after yourself
To do what you are told
And to respect me for who I am.

Issey King (10)
Holy Trinity Primary School, Maresfield Gardens

The Annoyed Football

I am tired of you.
Toe punting me in my chest
It kills me
And if I was you
I wouldn't do that to you.

I know
What you have been saying about the goalkeeper
And you're going to trick the goalkeeper so
You can win the match.

I have
Had it up to here with you popping me
And making me flat as a pancake, so next time
Don't be pounding me.

Jamie Murray (10)
Holy Trinity Primary School, Maresfield Gardens

Beautiful Rock

Look at that gleaming piece of rock, it looks so beautiful.
What kind of rock is that? It is on fire.
Look at that rock, it's so big!
Let's go to the park, let's play on the zip line
Or just play on the rock, it looks so beautiful.
Let's go on the zip line one million times.
Look at that long queue, it looks so long, so let's get moving.
Shall we go to the water park tomorrow?
I am so hot, I feel like a sizzling sausage.
So look at that rock, must look at that rock.
Don't stop! We can go to the beach and get some ice cream
Or let's float in the dinghy, till waves pull us down,
Or get a board - we can fly high on the waves,
Because we all want to fly like a bird
To reach that wonderful rock.
So look at that beautiful rock. *Just look!*

Charlie Elliott Acton (8)
Longshaw Primary School, Chingford

In The Morning Up I Rise

In the morning up I rise
Just to test my bleary eyes.

In the evening I go to bed
Just to rest my weary head.

In the afternoon I work so hard
Just to pay my credit card.

Holly Barnes (7)
Longshaw Primary School, Chingford

Brothers

B ad tempered
R eally silly
O rdinary
T easing
H urtful
E nemy
R ough
S aucy.

Daniella Giraldo (8)
Longshaw Primary School, Chingford

Bubblegum

Bubblegum is chewy,
Bubblegum is fun,
I want it all the time
So give me, give me some.

Tamara Watson (9)
Longshaw Primary School, Chingford

The Sizzly Sausage

Sizzly sausage, sizzly sausage
Sizzling in a pan
One got burnt and the other was alright.
Sizzly sausage, sizzly sausage
Getting hot, make it a bit cool
Sizzly sausage, sizzly sausage.

Rosie Grant (7)
Longshaw Primary School, Chingford

Seven Days

At first there was nothing, darkness, smoke,
No living creature 'til the Father spoke.

Then bursting, flaming, coming into sight,
Was God's greatest gift; dawn of light.

God created something high,
Which domed across the golden sky.

God created lots of sand
And He called it great land.

God made the sun, moon, stars,
Which glittered all around Mars.

God created whales, fish, birds,
Then birds were flying in great big herds.

God created animals on land
And humans were happy like he planned.

Then God rested
And he blessed it.

Sophie Hylands (8)
Our Lady & St Philip Neri RC Primary School, Sydenham

Seven Days

At first nothing but darkness and smoke,
Until the Father spoke.

Then bursting, flaming, coming into sight,
Was God's greatest gift, dawn of the light.

God created rainbows high swooping down from the sky
Passing by with the golden sun.

On the fourth day God created moon and stars,
Followed by Saturn and Mars.

Next God created birds and fish, whales
For the loving females and males.

Next God made mammals and plants,
Uncles and aunts.

God relaxed and blessed the world by looking at His work.

Isabelle Mullarkey (7)
Our Lady & St Philip Neri RC Primary School, Sydenham

A Poem About School

I was at school one day,
'Sit down,' the teacher would say.
'Everyone get out your recipe book,
Today we're going to learn how to cook.
Flatten your dough with a rolling pin,
It's a competition, who can win?
We're going to make chocolate cake,
Get a partner who knows how to bake.
Put it in the oven, ready to heat,
Whatever you do don't add meat.
When it is ready add whipped cream,
You over there, don't be mean.
Now take a slice,
Is it nice?'
It tastes great,
It's like heaven on a plate.

Isabella Nevin (10)
Our Lady & St Philip Neri RC Primary School, Sydenham

Seven Days

At first there was nothing, darkness, smoke
No living creature 'til the Father spoke.

Then bursting, flaming, coming into sight was
God's greatest gift; the dawn of light.

God created something high
Which arched across the golden sky.

God made the land and the plants
Through the wind the flowers danced.

God made the sun, moon and stars
These lovely lights to shine round Mars.

God made sea creatures, fish, birds
The lovely creatures fly in herds.

He made land creatures and the human beings
God enjoyed what He was seeing.

This is the day God had His rest,
This is the day the things got blessed.

Calvin Klobodu (8)
Our Lady & St Philip Neri RC Primary School, Sydenham

Dragon

D ragon with bat wings
R azor-sharp teeth like a flint knife
A dragon eats all flesh
G reat mammoth bird flying
O n his back he has buried spikes
N ever mess with a dragon!

Joshua Dent-Reynolds (8)
Our Lady & St Philip Neri RC Primary School, Sydenham

Seven Days

At first there was nothing, darkness, smoke
No living creature 'til the Father spoke.

Then bursting, flaming, coming into sight
Was God's greatest gift, the dawn of light.

God created something high
Which separated sea from sky.

Next God made
The land and plants.

Which everyone really
Loved and adored.

God created sun, moon and stars.
All of them still sitting on Mars.

Next God made fish and birds
Which sometimes got eaten like nerds.

Next God made mammals
Which are really animals.

Next God rested and kept on looking
Down at us.

Anthony Travell (8)
Our Lady & St Philip Neri RC Primary School, Sydenham

Seven Days

God made the light, that shines so bright.
God made the sky, that is up so high.
God made the plants, that can dance all the way to France.
God made the moon, when it was noon.
God made the fish, that can fit in a dish.
God made humans that can stand on land.
God rested, and the Devil didn't reject it.

Emmanuel Park (7)
Our Lady & St Philip Neri RC Primary School, Sydenham

Seven Days

At first there was nothing, darkness, smoke.
No living creature 'til the Father spoke.

Then bursting, flaming, coming into sight
Was God's greatest gift; the dawn of light.

God created the clouds so high,
Which was called the great white sky.

He made every plant on land.
He made it beautiful like He had planned.

He put the sun so close to Mars
And the moon so close to the stars.

God created sky so high,
So birds could fly in the great white sky.

God created animals on land
And humans were happy like He planned.

God had finished like He planned so He could rest,
But He was a little bit of a pest.

Charlie Joseph Carney (8)
Our Lady & St Philip Neri RC Primary School, Sydenham

The Cowboy

Over the steep hill the cowboy will ride
With spurs on his boots and a rope at his side
Through the Wild West he finds a way
For the little cowboy to hunt for his prey
He comes whirling his rope around his head
Catches the thieves with only one hand
Work now is over, he gallops away
His horse obeys the route in which he says
Through the mounted trees he straddles away
For the little cowboy to find the place where he stays.

Jason Jouan (10)
Our Lady & St Philip Neri RC Primary School, Sydenham

Seven Days

At first there was nothing; darkness, smoke,
No living creature, 'til the Father spoke.

Then bursting, flaming, coming into sight
Was God's greatest gift; the dawn of light.

God created sky and sea.
Sea was below and a rainbow sky was high.
He made bright yellow sunflowers.

God planted seeds into His vineyard
And waited. He grew passion flowers,
Which went to Mars.

God created burning sun and it was day.
He also made the white moon and called it night.
He put the stars with the bright moon.

God made blazing golden sky with small birds
As a group in the background flew
In the blazing shiny sky.

God made little teeny weenie fish
In the glistening sea and we call it ocean.

God made lovely big yellow sand on beautiful lands
With land animals and humans.
He also made mammals on a lovely cheerful land
And God made animals for us. Hooray for God.

On the last day God
Rested after all that
Hard work.

Theo Johns (8)
Our Lady & St Philip Neri RC Primary School, Sydenham

Seven Days

At first there was nothing; darkness, smoke.
No living creature 'til the Father spoke.

Then bursting, flaming, coming into sight,
Was the greatest gift; the dawn of light.

He separated the sea from a gift so high,
It was a huge dome called the sapphire sky.

It separated the sea from the clouds up there,
So the sky was visible everywhere.

On the third day God created plants
And the powerful breeze made the flowers dance.

God created land that same day,
To help the plants grow, breathe and sway.

On the fourth day, He made moon and sun,
To have some more light for His plans to come.

He also created the small white stars
To light the enormous planet Mars!

God then made creatures, whales and fish,
To roam the ocean, sway and swish.

Then he made birds to sing and fly,
Across the great big dome, the sky.

God made animals to travel the Earth,
Then there was another big birth!

He made a human, just like himself,
With happiness, hands and all His wealth.

So God had finished the Earth at last,
He thought He'd worked very fast.

So He rested a lot on that day
And He thought, everything was OK.

Aaron Akpojaro (7)
Our Lady & St Philip Neri RC Primary School, Sydenham

Seven Days

At first there was nothing, darkness, smoke.
No living creatures 'til the Father spoke.

Then bursting, flaming, coming into sight,
Was God's greatest gift; the dawn of light.

God created something high
Which separated sea from sky.

It was the third day and He created land
And He did it by His own hand.

On the fourth day He created the sun, stars and moon,
While He hummed a lovely tune.

The fifth day it was and He created monsters,
Just like big fat lobsters.

It was the sixth day and He created humans and animals,
Some of the animals were birds, fish and camels.

The seventh day it was and He created nothing, but rested
Then He looked back and He blessed it.

Liam Cavanagh (8)
Our Lady & St Philip Neri RC Primary School, Sydenham

Henry VIII

Henry was so smart, so bright,
His jewels shone like the shining light.
He was crowned in 1509
And loved to eat food and drink wine.

Henry became fatter and fatter,
So exercising did not matter.
Henry had one boy and two girls,
His clothing was decorated in beautiful swirls.

Henry loved to write poetry,
He would say, 'No one's better than me.'
Henry died in a very sad way,
But at least we remember him still today.

Shareen Ffrench (10)
Our Lady & St Philip Neri RC Primary School, Sydenham

Seven Days

At first there was nothing; darkness, smoke
No living creature 'til the Father spoke.

Then bursting, flaming, coming into sight,
Was God's greatest gift; the dawn of light.

God created a sapphire up high,
Which separated the sea from the sky.

God created lots of land
And near the sea He put some sand.

On the fourth day God made the sun
Then he started to have some fun.

Whales and fish He threw into the sea,
Tomorrow He is gonna make me.

On the sixth day God made mammals
And in the desert He put some camels.

On the seventh day God started to rest
He had truly done His best.

Kitty Walker (8)
Our Lady & St Philip Neri RC Primary School, Sydenham

Seven Days

At first there was nothing; darkness, smoke,
No living creature 'til the Father spoke.

Then bursting, flaming, coming into sight,
Was God's greatest gift; the dawn of light.

God created the dome so high,
With sea divided with the sky.

Time flying past and by,
All through the home-made sky.

Then came plants
And they made a little dance.

With land as well God started to get planned
To get ready for a piece of bladed land.

On Mars there was the village of Pars,
With the stars and moon doing a lovely tune
With the boiling hot sun and the Earth like a hot bun

Birds flying high,
Way up in the sky.
All the fish in an enormous dish,
Which was the sea where animals swam free.

Now the humans came like God again,
With land animals and sugarcane.
Lovely animals prancing and dancing,
With nature in its place for glancing.

God resting under a tree said,
'This is the life people will live.'
With all the people munching up their chives.

Stephanie Hilbig (8)
Our Lady & St Philip Neri RC Primary School, Sydenham

Seven Days

At first there was nothing; darkness, smoke
No living creature 'til the Father spoke.

Then bursting flames, coming into sight
Was God's greatest gift; the dawn light.

He separated sea from sky
Which arched across the golden sky.

He started planting daffodil seeds
In the garden they turned into weeds.

Every morning there is a bright sun
And a moon to shine upon everyone.

It was the sixth day and He created humans and animals
Some animals; lambs, birds and mammals.

God rested on the last day
He saw everybody so He went to play.

Stephany Hernandez (9)
Our Lady & St Philip Neri RC Primary School, Sydenham

Seven Days

God created the golden sky
God created the high sky
God created the sun and moon high
God created the sea and bright stars
God created dark and light
God created the land
On the seventh day
He rested and looked
At the beautiful things
He had done
And it was wonderful.

Chloe Sandley
Our Lady & St Philip Neri RC Primary School, Sydenham

Seven Days

At first there was nothing; darkness, smoke
No living creature 'til the Father spoke.

Then bursting, flaming, coming into sight
Was God's greatest gift; the dawn of light.

God created something high
Which arched across the golden sky.

God created land and plants
Scattered daisies across by chance.

God created moon, sun and stars
God put the moon next to Mars.

God created sea monsters, fish and birds
Which gathered up into herds.

God created animals on land, and people
Then God let them rule the Earth of children and pupils.

Then God rested and had a nice relax
'Til the people had a bad tax.

Laura Burns (7)
Our Lady & St Philip Neri RC Primary School, Sydenham

The Haunted House

Paul walked in with a great big *bang!*
After he did the door went *slam.*
The stairs went *creak,*
The house was very weak.

The walls were dark,
Then he heard a bark.
Woof, woof, it was a dog,
In the fog.

He went up the stairs,
Then he saw a row of chairs.
He caught an eye on a coffin
Then he heard someone coughing.

Ahh! What was that?
It was a huge cat.
He ran from the house,
Then that was that.
That was the legend of the haunted house.

John Costello (10)
Our Lady & St Philip Neri RC Primary School, Sydenham

Happiness

Happiness is like the sun coming out on a beautiful day.
Happiness is like a box of chocolates that have been given to you.
Happiness looks like lovely roses which have just been planted.
Happiness feels like a smile which has been put on your
face by the Holy Spirit.
Happiness smells like freshly baked bread.
Happiness is blue like the sea.
Happiness is black hair like ebony.
Happiness is like whales splashing in the ocean.
Happiness smells like my mum's perfume
Which just makes me happy.

Susan Uwah (10)
Our Lady & St Philip Neri RC Primary School, Sydenham

The Seven Ages Of Woman

(With thanks to William Shakespeare)

All the world's a stage
And all the men and women merely players;
They have their exits and their entrances,
And one woman in her time plays many parts,
Her act being seven ages.
First of all the infant, crying and sobbing for her mother;
Then a loving schoolgirl walking to school,
But chatting in class
And then annoyed at boys taunting her,
But still looking for more whilst putting on make-up,
Using her secret touch.
Then, a housewife, full of weariness, hair in curls,
Jealous of career women, sullen and depressed,
Trying to keep her children healthy, still going through stress
And then, the pillar of the community,
In fair, slim body, eating hardly any meat.
Eyes severe, hair short and smartly permed,
Wise and full of modern ideas, caring for the environment
And she is still able to play her part.
The sixth age shifts into smaller trousers that are
                              growing too big for her,
With glasses on her nose and bag on her side,
Her confident voice faded and become weak with sorrow.
Last scene of all that ends this strange eventful history
Is second childishness and near oblivion,
With false teeth, contact lenses, dulled tastebuds,
There's not much left of her!

Jessie Grace Cooney (10)
Our Lady & St Philip Neri RC Primary School, Sydenham

Happiness

Happiness is the yellow sun
Peeping through the blue sky
It smells like my mum's new perfume
Happiness tastes like an
Everlasting gobstopper, so sweet.
Feels like God has made me alive.
Happiness looks like a bright,
Green bud beginning new life.
You hear it, people are laughing.
Happiness feels like you can let
Your beautiful face smile.
Tastes like sweets, never melts
In your mouth.
Happiness smells like flowers with
The scent of lavender.
The things that make me happy are
My loveable family and
My best friend Victoria.

Natasha Adomako (10)
Our Lady & St Philip Neri RC Primary School, Sydenham

PE Lessons

PE is a rush to get changed
PE is having the right games kit
PE is the time to take your jewellery off
PE is the time to exercise

PE is waiting for a game to begin
PE you go and enjoy the fun
PE you must have won
PE is for all

PE is cool
PE is great
We should have PE every day.

Ronnie Odlum (10)
Our Lady & St Philip Neri RC Primary School, Sydenham

Seven Days

At first there was nothing; darkness, smoke
No living creature 'til the Father spoke.

Then bursting, flaming, coming into sight
Was God's greatest gift; the dawn of light.

God created clouds up high
Which was the grand golden sky.

God created plants on land
And put the world on top of His hand.

God created sun, moon and stars
And made the world His Mars.

God created sea monsters, whales, fish and birds
And animals which have lots of fur.

God created animals and humans on land
And made a big band.

God rested
Until three days were up.

Milly Odlum (8)
Our Lady & St Philip Neri RC Primary School, Sydenham

Autumn

Autumn leaves falling like
bristly conkers plummeting to the ground

Autumn leaves falling like
acorns pinged down by the squirrels

Autumn leaves falling like
crunchy, crispy crisps

Autumn leaves falling like
wrinkled pieces of paper

Autumn leaves falling like
squirrels leaping from the branches

Autumn sounds whistling like
the bone-chilling autumn winds

Autumn colours appearing like
a beautiful painting coming to life

Autumn scenes of emptiness like
a solitary autumn street

Autumn trees bare, stretching their
naked branches up towards the clouds

Autumn, one of the many seasons
but just the same as the others - coming round again and again.

Sean Fowley (10)
Our Lady & St Philip Neri RC Primary School, Sydenham

The Dream

Every night I have a funny dream,
But tonight I'm hoping for none to be seen.
My mum kisses me goodnight
Like I'm going far away.
I shut my eyes and squeeze them tight
And for the rest I have to pray.

I start to drift off
I'm swirling around
Then I suddenly appear in my school playground
This is crazy . . . wait . . .
What's that sound . . . ?
Creak . . . stomp . . . stomp.

It's my teacher telling me off
She is coming, what should I do?
I shut my eyes and squeeze them tight
And *poof!*

She turns into a mouse
I grabs her quick
She bites my lip
So I shut my eyes and squeeze them tight
I wake up really quick
Squeak! Squeak!
I find a mouse on my lap
Oh no, it's my teacher!

Hannah Louise Smith (10)
Our Lady & St Philip Neri RC Primary School, Sydenham

World War II

Smash! Boom!
It spelt out doom.
The bombs fell down,
I panicked and looked around.
The noise was deafening
I was confused. What was happening?

I ran and ran, but the noise got closer,
Turning around,
Looking at the town,
Smashed, bashed,
Crashed, lashed,
It was mashed.

I decided to investigate,
I went through the town's main gate.
I looked at all the devastation,
I really needed a vacation.
Looking for people who were alive,
I was sad, I started to cry.

Bang, bang I'm dead,
Two bullets in my head.

Kieran Cavanagh (10)
Our Lady & St Philip Neri RC Primary School, Sydenham

Art

Art is when the sun is in the sky
the landscape magical
a place where you can fly.

Art is a mirror reflecting thought
a moment in history
where imagination is caught.

Art is freedom
a time to enjoy
more fun and pleasure than any toy.

Art is when you learn
other artists inspire
and you make up your own art.

Art is where you do different designs
like patterns
a hard design or different lines.

If you make a birthday card for a friend
you can use art to show how much you care
your art is always there to share.

Only art can truly show what a place really looks like
a description can give clues
but sometimes they are not right.

When you finish your work
it's time for display
bringing joy to the world, nothing else to say.

Olamide Somade (10)
Our Lady & St Philip Neri RC Primary School, Sydenham

Right And Wrong

Is it right to pick your nose?
Is it right to touch your toes?
Is it wrong to mess about?
Is it wrong to have a doubt?

Is it right to kick a ball?
Is it right to knock down a wall?
Is it wrong to swim in the ocean?
Is it wrong to walk in slow motion?

Is it right to steal from a shop?
Is it right to just lay down or flop?
Is it wrong to brush your hair?
Is it wrong to capture a bear?

Is it right to jump up and down?
Is it right to take the Queen's crown?
Is it wrong to shout at your mum?
Is it wrong to say, 'You're dumb!'

Jessica Ball (10)
Our Lady & St Philip Neri RC Primary School, Sydenham

Art

Art is a line on a piece of paper
Art is a tone of colour
Art can be brighter or duller
Art is a splatter
Art can make people look thin or fatter
Art is like a delicate butterfly
Art can be sad, it can make me cry.

I like to draw planes taking off in flight
I like to draw anything in my sight
Art is a blob of paint
Colour can be light, it can be really faint
Art brightens up a room in the morning sun
Art is a gift for the talented ones.

Leanne Gale King (10)
Our Lady & St Philip Neri RC Primary School, Sydenham

A Bird

A bird from north,
Helped some people forth.
It led them to a house,
In the shape of a mouse.
The interrupted people saw,
A boy who was four.
The boy led them in,
With a surprised grin.
To their amazement,
He led them to the basement.
They stayed there till late,
Until they realised their fate.
The boy went away
And let them stay.
They were about to finish their life,
The husband and the wife.

Sam Mills (10)
Our Lady & St Philip Neri RC Primary School, Sydenham

The Silver Fish

While I was fishing,
By the sea,
I caught a silver fish
Named Lee.
He pleaded me
To set him free.
But I said, *'No,*
I won't let go.'
The silver fish
Offered a wish,
Only if he
Could be set free.
So I whispered my wish
And it came true.
I had silver fish stew.

Jordan Akpojaro (11)
Our Lady & St Philip Neri RC Primary School, Sydenham

The Young Evacuee

I can see sadness on parents' faces,
As I leave shore to new land,
I see planes darting and speeding,
Like there is no tomorrow,
As I sit down with sorrow.

I can feel the vibrations of bombs,
As they light up the night sky and
Lash in the ground with much debris.
I also feel lonely and frightened,
For what might happen next.
I question myself for answers.

I can hear people shouting and screaming
Injured people that is.
I hear ambulances and the fire brigade
Coming to help survivors at their worst.

As I pack, I see the photo
Of my father and mother only
Now waiting in suspense.
As I pack, I fold my clothes.

When I arrive home,
I see many things are different.
Everywhere I went to,
It's all vanished or been bombed, one or the other.

Ann-Marie Whelan (9)
Our Lady & St Philip Neri RC Primary School, Sydenham

The Silver Salmon

While fishing in the deep, blue lake,
I caught a lovely silver salmon,
'Me man!' quoth he,
'Please set me free, I'll grant you a free golden wish!
A tower of gold? A million pounds,
Or the newest rod, unbreakable?'
I commented, 'OK . . .' and let him go,
But he laughed at me and he shot off
And left me, here, in the silent breeze
To talk to the sea.

Later I caught the fish again.
(the heavenly king of salmon)
And once more he offered me,
If I would gently set him free,
He said I could have three more wishes,
If I threw him back to the fishes.
But he was delectable . . .

Thomas Hilbig (10)
Our Lady & St Philip Neri RC Primary School, Sydenham

Happiness

Happiness is yellow like the sun on a beautiful day.
Happiness tastes like a box of chocolates that are melting.
Happiness looks like fair flowers budding and growing happily.
Happiness smells like a warm roast dinner that is steaming.
Happiness feels like a smile that you have received from a friend.
Happiness is orange like a bright light shining on you.
Happiness is like countries who were at war but have peace.
Happiness smells like the air when it is fresh and clean.
Happiness feels like your blood is being warmed up by a friend.

Katie-Louise Shepherd Gill (10)
Our Lady & St Philip Neri RC Primary School, Sydenham

School Bus

The school bus is rusty
The school bus is musty

There's gum under the seats
And old dirty sweets

As the bus trugs along
They sing a boring, silly song

And draw dumb pictures
While telling giddy fixtures

There's an odd stinky smell
From a girl called Mel.

A gang of nasty boys,
That make lots of noise.

The school bus is clusty,
The school bus is dusty.

Told you it was yucky.

Mitchell Roy Burns (10)
Our Lady & St Philip Neri RC Primary School, Sydenham

It Wasn't Me, It Was Him!

While waiting in the bitter grounds,
I was caught sneaking into class by Mr Nift
And he mumbled to me, 'My girl,' whispered he,
'Please get me my paperwork and I'll give you a gift:
A head teacher's award? A big juicy steak?
A great extra hour, instead of a small rainy break!'
So, I said, 'OK,' and grabbed the paper,
But Sir just giggled at me as he sprinted away,
And left me to get in trouble by Mrs Kaper.

Today I got caught again,
(To get heated up in a heated room),
And once again, Mr Nift offered me,
If only I would get the key,
Any number of special prizes,
Or get a burst of hidden surprises.

He got detention, then the sack.

Jessica Baxter (9)
Our Lady & St Philip Neri RC Primary School, Sydenham

Seven Days

At first there was nothing; darkness, smoke.
No living creation 'til the Father spoke.
Then bursting, flaming, coming into sight
Was God's creations, the land and most lovely plants.
God created the hen and made animals.
God created the moon and stars so beautiful
And high in the sky.
God created the humans and the ponies and tigers,
God rested and did no more.

Shannon Edwards (7)
Our Lady & St Philip Neri RC Primary School, Sydenham

The Green Fish

While hunting in the deep dark rainforest,
I caught a hissing snake
And he said to me, 'My girl set me free,'
'What's in it for me?'
'I'll grant you a wish;
A palace of gold, or a wishing fish?'
And with a smile on my face,
I replied with a, 'Yes,' and set him free,
But he giggled at me as he slithered away
And left me hissing my wish
Into a silent forest.

Today I caught that snake once again
(That slimy green prince of snakes)
And once again he offered me,
If I would set him free,
Any one of a number of wishes
If I would put him back in the bushes.
He was scrumptious.

Paige Holdaway (9)
Our Lady & St Philip Neri RC Primary School, Sydenham

Evacuees

You can send me away
And you won't have to pay.
I don't get it
Because I can't fit all
My clothes in my suitcase.

I feel the pain,
As I get on a train.
I feel the heat of my parents
As they wave.
Where are they going?

I see the planes going past,
Extremely fast.
They might have had a crash
With a big bash!
I see fire, oh no!

I hear bombs colliding
Into ground,
With a pound.
I hear the crackling
And then *bang.*

I'm coming home,
To soak in foam.
I hope my dad is there,
Otherwise I will be in despair.
He's not there, who will I stay with?

Callum Fransen (10)
Our Lady & St Philip Neri RC Primary School, Sydenham

The Green Trout

While fishing in the deep, dark lagoon
I caught a lovely green trout
And he spoke to me, 'My dear girl,' bellowed he
'Please set me free and I'll grant your wish
A world of treasure? A castle of silver
Or all your mind can hold?'
And I said, 'OK,' and I set him free
But he giggled at me as he swam away
And left me singing my wish
Into a quiet blue ocean

Today I caught that lovely trout again
(That lovely green prince of trouts)
And once again he suggested to me
Any one of a number of wishes
If I would throw him back to the fishes
He was yum.

Chelsey-Ann Yousif (10)
Our Lady & St Philip Neri RC Primary School, Sydenham

Seven Days

At first there was nothing; darkness, smoke
No living creature until the Father spoke.

Then bursting, flaming, coming into sight
Was God's greatest gift; the dawn of light.

God created a rainbow up high
Which arched across the light blue sky.

Then God made something nice
It was the Earth and plants
This was the fourth day I liked.

Then God made the sun, the moon and stars
That shine nicely in the sky.
That was the fifth day I liked.

Then God made humans to rule the Earth
And animals, that was the sixth day I liked.

On the seventh day He rested!

Pearle Morha (8)
Our Lady & St Philip Neri RC Primary School, Sydenham

Friends Forever

I was at school one day
And saw the new girl, her name was Faye.
We became friends, very good friends,
She said the friendship would never end.
Together we went out at break,
We giggled so much, we got an ache.
After fifteen minutes, the whistle blew,
Faye fell over and hit her nose.
I took her to the school hospital,
Then as a treat, I took her to the mall.
We had lunch in McDonald's café,
We went back to school, it was the end of the day.
After school, I went to her house,
Her mum fed Hilary, their pet mouse.
We did our homework in her room,
She said I could sleep over, I was over the moon.
I went back home to get my things,
For supper, we had chicken wings.
We played the game, 'Truth or dare',
Then when she wasn't looking, I pulled her hair.
We had our feast at midnight,
Tasty chocolates in the shape of a kite.
Faye's mum tucked us up in bed,
'Goodnight little girlies,' she softly said.
I went to sleep without another word,
Because I was tired, my vision blurred.
The next day we went back to school,
Avoiding the new swimming pool.
I slept over that day too,
I knew Mum was missing me, boo hoo, boo hoo!

Samantha Tuckey
Our Lady & St Philip Neri RC Primary School, Sydenham

The Evacuees

You can see the evacuees on the train
They are obviously in pain.
Looking at the country, what a bore,
Thinking of their families back in the war.

They are not hungry,
But very angry.
Not feeling glad,
But feeling sad.

They look really bad,
Also very mad.
Hugging their teddies,
Keeping their minds nice and steady.

The train is going faster,
They are thinking of their headmaster.
Their families still love them
Hopefully they will get to see them again.

Ruairi O'Connor (9)
Our Lady & St Philip Neri RC Primary School, Sydenham

A Poem About School

I don't like school
The only good thing about it is football
I had to look
Inside the answer book
For some answers
About some dancers
I had lots of detentions
For not paying attention
In the playground someone tried to be cool
I said to him, 'Don't be a fool.'

At playtime it got worse and worse
I fell over and had to go to the school nurse
In school dinners I had fish
After lunch we had to do English
Someone tried to commit a crime
But Miss caught him in the nick of time
I got lots of homework
My sister was being a jerk
I woke up, it was all a dream
I had to do this day again, it made me scream.

Jack Amphlett (10)
Our Lady & St Philip Neri RC Primary School, Sydenham

Evacuee Sadness

I can see the sorrow on parents' faces
Tears drizzling down their pale white traces.
As I set aboard
I praise to the Lord.

As I sit down I can hear bombs landing
I can see troops surrounding.
As I get comfy I feel something pointy,
The loose screw that was jointy.

The passenger next to me offered me a sweet
And a slab of meat.
When I left the train
I saw a plane.

As I lined up
Someone had a cut.
I got picked by a farmer
Who did drama.

When it was all over
I went back to Dover.
I saw my dad
And he had an arm pad.

Benjamin Samuel (9)
Our Lady & St Philip Neri RC Primary School, Sydenham

Seven Days

At first there was nothing; darkness, smoke,
No living creature 'til the Father spoke.

Then burning, flaming, coming into sight,
Was God's greatest gift; the dawn of light.

God created clouds up high
Which arched across the golden sky.

God created land and plants
To have a quick glance.

God created sun, moon and sky
The sun, moon and sky were very high.

God created sea creatures, fishes, birds
God made the powerful words.

God created land and beast
God had a big bright feast.

God created sea creatures and fish
He had supper on His bright clean dish

And on the last day He rested.

Jack Trype (8)
Our Lady & St Philip Neri RC Primary School, Sydenham

The Creation

At first there was nothing; darkness, smoke
No living creatures 'til the Father spoke.

Then bursting, flaming, coming into sight
Was God's greatest gift; the dawn of light.

God created something high
Which separated the sea from the sky.

God created with His hand
All the plants living on the land.

God created sun, moon and stars up high
Which shines and glitters in the sky.

God created birds and fishes
That we ate on dishes.

God created the animals on land
And human beings.

God had a rest and the world was finished.

Lydia Agui (7)
Our Lady & St Philip Neri RC Primary School, Sydenham

Seven Days

At first there was nothing; darkness, smoke,
No living creatures 'til the Father spoke.

Then bustling, flaming, coming into sight
Was God's greatest gift; the dawn of light.

God separated sea from sky
With passing way up high.

God made the land and the plants
Grow in the bright sun and dance.

God made the sun, it comes in the day
And the moon and stars come in the night
To light our path and show the way.

God made the birds that fly high
And the fish that swim by.

God made the animals and
Made the humans to rule the world.

God created no more on the last day.

Amy Elliott (7)
Our Lady & St Philip Neri RC Primary School, Sydenham

Seven Days

At first there was nothing; darkness, smoke,
No living creature 'til the Father spoke.

Then bursting, flaming, coming into sight
Was God's greatest gifts; the dawn of light.

God created something high
Which was the great bright sky.

It was the third day and along came land
Plants were created by God's hand.

Then next came sun which ruled the day,
Also the moon and stars which ruled night when you lay.

It was the fifth day and fish swam
And then sea creatures' birth began.

It was the sixth day and we were born
Including humans which woke up at dawn.

God's work was over while He rested
He sat there and watched His creations and blessed it.

Joseph Dave Gomez (8)
Our Lady & St Philip Neri RC Primary School, Sydenham

Seven Days

At first there was nothing; darkness, smoke
No living creatures 'til the Father spoke.

Then bursting, flaming, coming into sight,
God's greatest gift; the dawn of light.

He created a dome up above high,
And separated the sea from sky.

Then He created a beautiful land
That had been covered in plants and sand.

After He created sun, moon and stars,
Which travelled around from this planet to Mars.

Then He created sea monsters and birds,
Which amazingly came forth in God's words.

Last He created animals and humans on land,
That travelled all over hills and sand.

Then He rested from the seven days,
And we all give thanks with joy and praise.

Ebamiyo Somade (8)
Our Lady & St Philip Neri RC Primary School, Sydenham

Seven Days

At first there was darkness, smoke;
No living thing 'til the Father spoke.

Then bursting, flaming, coming into sight
Was God's greatest gift; the dawn of light.

God created clouds high
Which was the glittering golden sky.

The spiky grass and the wooded land
The colourful flowers and the yellow sand.

The yellow sun burning bright.
The moon and stars twinkled at night.

God created silver fishes and birds
Every colour you could wish.

God created human beings
Who could express their own feelings.

God rested on the last day
And smiled at all the days gone past.

Hayley Sandley (7)
Our Lady & St Philip Neri RC Primary School, Sydenham

The Brown Rabbit

While hunting in the damp forest,
I caught a cuddly brown rabbit
And he spoke to me, 'My girl,' said he,
'Please set me free, I'll grant you a wish
A cute goldfish? A sack full of money?'
I said, 'OK,' and I set him free,
But he chatted at me and hopped away
And left me murmuring my wish into a green bush.

Today I caught that rabbit again
(that lovely brown prince of rabbits)
And once again he offered me
If I would only set him free,
Any of a number of wishes
If I would throw him back into the forest
He was delectable.

Harriet Maddison (9)
Our Lady & St Philip Neri RC Primary School, Sydenham

The Sun

The sun is like a burning fire,
It makes your ice cream melt,
It melts your chocolate all the time,
So you should eat it quick.

The sun makes you hot so,
You start to sweat,
It makes you hot all the time,
So it feels like you're going to melt.

You notice the sun's about to go,
Because the moon comes up,
And it gets cooler
And becomes night.

April Padulla (7)
Oxford Gardens Primary School, Oxford Gardens

Pancake

Put some butter in the pan
(Scoop butter out of the pot)
Make sure it isn't from a can
(Wave your right finger)
After break the butter up
(Pretend to put the cooker on)
After get some honey
(Pretend to scoop some honey on the pancake)
And then bake it again.

(Turn the oven on)
Now you canfldip the pancake
(Pretend to flip the pancake)
Now cut the pancake
(Pretend to cut the pancake)
And now you can eat your pancake
(Pretend to eat the pancake).

Ahmad Alshibani
Oxford Gardens Primary School, Oxford Gardens

The Wind

There is a sound in the house,
That sounds like a wolf,
That makes the London Eye move,
It's terrifying
And it makes me shake
The wolf was out of breath.

The wind rattles the windows
With its nightly breeze,

In the morning
He runs away at last
Huffing and puffing
The wind.

Mason Roseboom (7)
Oxford Gardens Primary School, Oxford Gardens

Pizza

Put some butter on a plate
(Make butter, then put on a plate)
Make sure to invite your mate
(Pretend to have a telephone)
Put some flour in a bowl
(Pretend to put flour in a bowl)
Now to go and score a goal
(Pretend to score a goal)
Now we make the dough
(I knead the dough)
Tell your mate not to go
(Say no)
Put the toppings on top
(Pretend to put toppings on)
Now get some fizzy pop
(Get fizzy pop)
Now I am showing my drool
(Spit drool)
Get the cheese and pull
(Pretend to pull).

Alia Hassan (8)
Oxford Gardens Primary School, Oxford Gardens

The Wind

The wind is a wolf,
That runs all day,
Never stops howling getting bored all day.

He goes round all day and all night,
He runs wild every day,
Until you don't notice him.

Then in the morning he scampers away,
Always huffing always puffing,
My friend the wind.

Zakaria Nawhi (7)
Oxford Gardens Primary School, Oxford Gardens

My Friend Sam

My best friend is Sam,
His girlfriend is Pam.

His favourite player is Rooney,
And he likes to be loony.

His favourite team is Man U,
And he likes to fan you.

He likes to eat out of a can,
And he likes to eat jam.

He likes his gran,
He likes to have a fan.

His hair is brown,
He wants a crown.

He climbs up trees,
And sees lots of bees.

He saw a nest,
And said it was the best.

Max Payne (8)
Oxford Gardens Primary School, Oxford Gardens

The Wind

On windy nights like this,
The bricks fall down,
Crashing hard to the ground.
Sometimes it makes me laugh,
I find it quite funny when people fall over
And land on their tummies, ha, ha.
When I get home I have a nice cup of tea,
It makes me feel sleepy,
So I get into bed and fall asleep.

Roxanne Hughes (7)
Oxford Gardens Primary School, Oxford Gardens

My Friend Alia

My friend Alia
Has a sister called Salia

He plays in the park
He lives on an ark

I'm his best friend
Our friendship will never end

I go to his house
His cat ate a mouse

His favourite food is ham
His dad drives a van

He never tells a lie
And neither do I.

Bertie Gillbert (8)
Oxford Gardens Primary School, Oxford Gardens

My Kennings Poem

Stinky smeller
Loud snorer
Mud lover
Ugly looker
Plant eater
Noise maker
Hot blooder
Weak lifter
Long sleeper
Good memoriser
Violent player
What animal could I be?

Answer: a pig.

Yogo Soto-Andre (8)
Oxford Gardens Primary School, Oxford Gardens

Here Comes A . . .

Here comes a ghost
He knocks over a post

Here comes a postman
And hits the ghost with a frying pan

Here comes the police
And his car is full of grease

Here comes a cat
With a funky hat

He acts like a frog
And jumps on a log

After this they have a fight
It will not finish, oh, it's night

Here comes a staff
Who stopped at a café.

Jamal Mohammed (8)
Oxford Gardens Primary School, Oxford Gardens

Miss Stapleton

She rolls her eyes at me
(Rolls her eyes)

She gets angry
(Puts on an angry face)

She's sometimes happy
(Puts on a happy face)

She's sometimes fun
(Puts on a fun face)

She goes mad
(Puts on a mad face).

Danni Anicic (8)
Oxford Gardens Primary School, Oxford Gardens

The Wind

The wind is a dog
A dog that's howling
Makes a loud sound
A sound with its mouth.

At night you can't see
See anything scary
But your ears hear the sound
Close the window
Or tuck yourself in
You will never stop hearing it.

It will now go, go far away
Go to outer space, never to be seen
To never ever be seen
But only on *Mars*.

Adam Moussa (7)
Oxford Gardens Primary School, Oxford Gardens

A Tour Of A Bus Garage

One time I entered a bus garage
with my grandad, just us.
Lots of hard workers, young and old.
I went in even more and I got told that
to be a bus driver, and learn more,
to get in the cab door
and feel the bus' floor.
Then I went up to the third floor
and saw even more,
I went down one floor
to where I'd never been before.
As I said goodbye,
my mouth went all dry.

Bradley McQueen (8)
Oxford Gardens Primary School, Oxford Gardens

The Wind

The wind is like an owl
Twittering away,
And nobody knows
What the owl will say.

The owl flies around
Spreading the message,
'Oh, oh, my twittering
Is the dread of the age.'

Another time the owl says,
'Hurry up, night animals, it's nearly day,
Search all around
And fetch your prey!'

Then, when the sun is coming up
And the sky is red,
The little, noisy owl
Has to go to bed.

Siqi Li (7)
Oxford Gardens Primary School, Oxford Gardens

My Best Friend

My best friend is called Terry
She's very smelly.

She acts very cheeky
And she's very freaky.

She gets in a lot of trouble
And her tummy always rumbles.

She's not very sporty
Her sister is called Courtney.

Her birthday was today
In the month of May.

Amane Gumaa (8)
Oxford Gardens Primary School, Oxford Gardens

Ancient Egypt

Get a dead body on the table
and take out the brain with a hook.
Have you ever seen such a thing in all your life?
Now twist the hook left and right.
Tip the body sideways to let the brains slip out into a ball.
Now take out the organs and put them into jars,
but be careful not to take the heart out.

Octavia Aspinall-Murray (9)
Oxford Gardens Primary School, Oxford Gardens

A Tornado

A tornado is like an onion.
It sounds like a lion roaring.
It starts to sound like lightning.
It starts to sound like thunder.
It starts to sound like lions growling.

Chad Grant (8)
Oxford Gardens Primary School, Oxford Gardens

The Rain

The rain is like a blackbird,
It whistles all night and it creeps through the light.
It moves quickly and it shouts,
The leaves are very angry, they fly every time.

Riad Nacir (7)
Oxford Gardens Primary School, Oxford Gardens

Ancient Egypt - Haikus

Find a dead body
Put it on the table now
And take the bits out.

Bits go in the jars
Weigh the feather and the heart
Go to afterlife.

Victor Chi Chi (8)
Oxford Gardens Primary School, Oxford Gardens

Cat

Mice lover
Dog hater
Mouse hunter
Great scratcher
Sleep litter
Pillow fighter
Fast runner
Great prowler.

Kyrone Wilson (8)
Oxford Gardens Primary School, Oxford Gardens

The Rain

The rain sounds like someone batting a ball,
The rain is strong and powerful,
When it tries to hit you it breaks,
The rain is like someone spitting down from the sky,
When the rain starts, the rain comes down,
You can drink it.

Michael Conners (7)
Oxford Gardens Primary School, Oxford Gardens

Cold Gold

Amazing swimmer
Water lover

Tail swisher
Cold blooder

Egg layer
Bubble blower

Bad thinker
Fin flapper

Shiny skinner
What am I?

Answer: a fish.

Honor Virden (8)
Oxford Gardens Primary School, Oxford Gardens

Min

I've got a dog whose name is Min
As soon as she's out she wants to come in.

She growls,
She howls,
She bumps,
She thumps,
She paws,
She claws,

And finally Min gets in.

Sam Campbell (8)
Oxford Gardens Primary School, Oxford Gardens

Football

Kick a ball (pretend to kick a ball)
Try not to fall (balance on one leg)
Be very cruel (pretend to push someone)
Look very cool (be very cool)
Don't be a fool (wave finger around ear)
Don't commit crime (pretend to have a gun)
Don't get a fine (throw pieces of paper away)
Drink lots of wine (pretend to drink wine from a glass).

Rafe Moran (8)
Oxford Gardens Primary School, Oxford Gardens

My Kennings Poem

Bone catcher
Mean biter
Quick runner
Meat eater

Human lover
Great chaser
Good hunter

What am I?

Answer: a dog.

Jennefer Yanez (8)
Oxford Gardens Primary School, Oxford Gardens

Thunder And Lightning

Thunder and lightning is like a lion
Roaring at my window and stomping on my wall
And it wants to eat me up
Then crashes at my door.

Howard Cotis (7)
Oxford Gardens Primary School, Oxford Gardens

The Wind

The wind is like an angry dinosaur,
He stomps his feet and growls,
He runs faster and faster as he gets
Nearer to his prey.

When the wind gets stronger he is like
A dinosaur crashing through the trees,
Eventually he gets tired and slows down,
In the morning he is calm until
He needs to kill again.

Sebastian Mujica-Villarroel (7)
Oxford Gardens Primary School, Oxford Gardens

The Thunder

The thunder is like an angry giant,
He slams his feet on your house,
His anger rattles your house,
The next day he is in big trouble from his mum,
He is not allowed to eat sweets for 5 days,
And his cry is as loud as aeroplane bullets.

Max McKenzie-Watkins (7)
Oxford Gardens Primary School, Oxford Gardens

Thunder And Lightning

Thunder is like a ghost
The ghost tries to drive your house
If he drives it, when you wake up your house will be a mess
You will be in a different place
And he does it for an hour or two
When he is tired he goes to a different place.

Isaac Butterfield-Kendall (7)
Oxford Gardens Primary School, Oxford Gardens

The Colours In The Rainbow

Rainbows are so colourful,
When the rain stops and the sun
Comes out.

The butterfly stops hiding and
Comes out.

But as time goes
The rainbow goes,
But you can always see
The colour *blue.*

Jade Major (7)
Oxford Gardens Primary School, Oxford Gardens

The Wind

The wind is like a wolf,
He cries in your house,
He tries to creep into your house,
And our windows rattle in the house,
Making a rusty sound,
He breaks into the house,
And eats you up at night-time.

Jack Henderson (7)
Oxford Gardens Primary School, Oxford Gardens

The Wind

At night the wind rustles and hustles like a scary ghost in the dark.
The wind can walk to your door in the night.
He comes creeping up the stairs like the Devil.
He can fly up to your bedroom window.

David Gorham (7)
Oxford Gardens Primary School, Oxford Gardens

The Rain

The rain is like mini dustbin lids,
Clattering down from the sky,
If the sun comes out
They then combine to
Make a rainbow.

The rainbow is like a crowd of colourful butterflies
In the shape of a semi-circle,
But as the sun fades away, the butterflies fade away,
But the rain comes back and so does
The dark gloomy clouds, the children go home.

Ruqaiyah Javaid (8)
Oxford Gardens Primary School, Oxford Gardens

The Rain

The rain is like a horse, ridden in the night,
He clatters his feet,
Galloping around the woods
And in the end, he goes away,
To find another place to stay -
But he comes back another day.

Safiyyah Da Silva (8)
Oxford Gardens Primary School, Oxford Gardens

The Rain

The rain is like a hamster sniffing,
Like a horse walking on the pavement
The rain is like a horse eating hay
The rain looks like sprinkles dropping
And mostly like tiny balls falling.

Abdul Ellah Yassein (7)
Oxford Gardens Primary School, Oxford Gardens

Snow

Snow is like a horse walking down the road,
Snow is like a thousand raindrops coming down,
Snow is like a tiger running through 100 trees in a forest.
Snow is my favourite weather.
Snow is like a polar bear running through the snow.
Snow comes in the last month and that's
Why I like it so.

Oliver Christiansen (8)
Oxford Gardens Primary School, Oxford Gardens

The Sun

The sun is like a cheetah
The sun moves fast, you can't stop it
If you do, it will burn you
When you come out to play, the cheetah
Will make you hotter
You will be hotter than ever,
You will need some wind.

Kai Egbuniwe
Oxford Gardens Primary School, Oxford Gardens

The Nice Wind

The wind is like it's pushing you
This wind is bracing stuff
The wind is scratching the door
The wind is running to the house
The wind has stopped
And it is a good day.

Denis Mesic (7)
Oxford Gardens Primary School, Oxford Gardens

Snow Time

The snow is as white as a ghost
The snow is very bright
When you watch the snow you always want some toast
The snow is very light

The snow moves like a snail
The snow sounds like a ghost, howling at night
When the snow drops, it looks like a veil
The snow drops very bright.

Leila Lee-Posner (7)
Oxford Gardens Primary School, Oxford Gardens

Rainbow

The rainbow is like four colours in the sky,
Little drops dropping so hard.
The rainbow comes when you see rain and sun together.
You can see the colour blue, it is bright, it is because
The sky is blue.
The butterfly dislikes the rain.
Butterflies flap their wings so softly,
The colours remind me of a rainbow.

Siobhan Farr (7)
Oxford Gardens Primary School, Oxford Gardens

Thunder And Lightning

Thunder and lightning is like a lion
Roaring for his lunch and walking down the road
If he catches you, he will eat you for his lunch.

Dionne Godfrey (7)
Oxford Gardens Primary School, Oxford Gardens

Snow

The snow is like a polar bear
That scratches through the night
And every time you hear him,
He always wants a fight.

The polar bear eats fish
And says, 'It's *delishhh!*'
I think he will stop and calm down
And he will start his moaning again
With a frown.

Olivia Tomlin-Shaw (8)
Oxford Gardens Primary School, Oxford Gardens

Thunder

The thunder is like a lion, roaring in the skies,
The lightning is angry like a lion.
The lion is roaming like an eagle.

The wind is running, the thunder keeps on running,
The thunder keeps on getting faster,
The lightning too.
When the lion is tired, he howls like a bear,
The thunder stops and the lion is sleeping,
The sun comes out.

Carlos Pacheco Ona (7)
Oxford Gardens Primary School, Oxford Gardens

The Rain

The rain sounds like a tap, tapping on my bath.
I love the rain, jumping the puddles.
It makes my feet wet, but I don't care,
I will change my socks when I get out of there.

Isiah Ayo (7)
Oxford Gardens Primary School, Oxford Gardens

Thunder And Lightning

Thunder is like
A tiger roaring
At your door.
Moving very
Loudly, like
Thunder going
To crush you.
The lightning
Has stopped now.

George O'Brien-Rey (7)
Oxford Gardens Primary School, Oxford Gardens

The Snow

The snow is great fun but it's freezing when I land on my bum.
It's as white as a polar bear, as cold as ice.
I love playing in it, it feels so nice.
Making snowballs and snowmen,
I hope it never rains again.
The snow is my favourite type of weather,
It's fun and hardly ever comes.

Marie-Hélène Bennett-Henry (7)
Oxford Gardens Primary School, Oxford Gardens

The Ghost, Wind And Fog

There once was a ghost who lived in a tree,
he reminds me of the noisy wind, and the smudgy fog.
Flying around like the wind and the rain,
the fog is a bit scary when it's all smoky and it's in the rain.
In the fog I can't see, sometimes it's frightening
when I can't see.

Bushra Ennakhli (7)
Oxford Gardens Primary School, Oxford Gardens

Snow

The snow is like a bear, the bear feels
really soft like snow.
It moves like a slowcoach on the ice.
I travel for food, like fish and berries on the cold ice.
I go for a swim on the cold ice, I see fish and I eat it.
I swim and swim in the freezing cold water, the snow,
the ice is making me shiver.

Kiki Belton (7)
Oxford Gardens Primary School, Oxford Gardens

The Thunder

The thunder's like a big tiger creeping around for its prey,
Scratching and looking for something to scare,
Be careful it doesn't see you, it will get you when
You're not looking.
When the thunder goes, all the other animals
Will come out again.

Aaron Parmley (7)
Oxford Gardens Primary School, Oxford Gardens

The Rain

Rain is like a lion, it's knocking on my door,
tapping on my head, making me slip around on the floor.
It creeps everywhere, wherever I go it follows me all around.
It scares me when I'm in my room and I hear it
tapping on the ground.

Sadie Kotey (7)
Oxford Gardens Primary School, Oxford Gardens

Rainbow

A rainbow is like a butterfly
Which is bright and coloured.
She's calm, gentle, amazing and quiet.
She's a very good little rainbow, so don't scare her away.
As it gets warmer, she's at last coming out to play.
I would like her to be my friend,
So listen to her when she -
She decides to go home.

Muna Abdelrhman (7)
Oxford Gardens Primary School, Oxford Gardens

Poem

I don't like watching TV
Playing on the computer
Is for me.

And with James I like
Zapping TVs
And building computers
That's also for me.

Chad Beaman (8)
Rainbow Montessori School, West Hampstead

Blown Away

By the wind I was blown away,
The trees were in my way.
I didn't know where I was going
The wind was blowing so hard
The clouds were grey
And the sun was hiding.

Clara Sibaud (8)
Rainbow Montessori School, West Hampstead

Can You Keep A Secret?

Can you keep a secret?
Don't tell anyone.
I've got it and I don't know why!
That's right, I've got a crush, a silly crush
And don't ask me why!
Brown hair, blue eyes and I call him mine!
Oh, oh, oh!

He's a boy and I love him,
Breaks a new heart every day.
He's a boy and a good one
and I only hope he'll stay that way.
You'll never know if he'll show up,
He gives you plenty of trouble.
He's a boy and his name is *mine!*

Alabama Boatman (9)
Rainbow Montessori School, West Hampstead

The Sun And The Moon

The sun is golden,
Shines so bright
And goes away
To sleep at night.
The moon takes its place
And gets there at a great pace
And in the day it goes away.
Every day the sun comes out to play
It warms our pretty Earth
From the moment of our birth.

Lottie Madden (9)
Rainbow Montessori School, West Hampstead

Butterflies

Butterflies flying through the mid-summer day
Changing colour as they fly through the trees,
Making them shimmer like stars
In the mid-summer sky.
They fly into the flower beds.

Annabelle Mintz (7)
Rainbow Montessori School, West Hampstead

Leaves

Fly from the trees like butterflies
Flying from the sky
Changing colour as they go by
Over the hills and mountains all day long
Through the forest, all the way home.

Jasmine Bayliss (8)
Rainbow Montessori School, West Hampstead

Books

Books are yellow, books are green,
They are so colourful and nice to read.
They're small and big, big and small,
It doesn't matter, you can just read them.

Anete Grinberga (7)
Rainbow Montessori School, West Hampstead

Sweets

Sweets are yummy
But not so good for your tummy
They are sweet, they are sour
But they only live for an hour.

Madalyn Farley (8)
Rainbow Montessori School, West Hampstead

Holiday

My holiday is the best,
My holiday is such fun,
I meet friends on my holiday
If I go on my holiday, it's best for me.
I'm happy to go on holiday.
I go high,
I go low,
But home is where I go.

Elise McTamaney (8)
Rainbow Montessori School, West Hampstead

I Am An Espresso Coffee . . .

I am a stereo, noisy and jumpy,
I am a table, strong and steady.
I am a skyscraper, confident and tall,
I am a clown, fooling around.
I am an Espresso coffee, awake and alert.

I am a train, speedy and upbeat . . .
I am an elephant, heavy on my feet.

Stephanie Clarke (11)
St Andrew's RC Primary School, Streatham

Starvation

Hungry people
Little children dying
They need more help
Famine.

Miles Felix (10)
St Andrew's RC Primary School, Streatham

Monday's Child

Monday's child stays in bed
Tuesday's child hates to be led
Wednesday's child wants attention
Thursday's child gets detention
Friday's child always screams
Saturday's child eats ice creams,
But the child that is born on the Sabbath Day
Has a lot to explain and say.

Daniel J Edwards (10)
St Andrew's RC Primary School, Streatham

Scaly Slitherer

Sand creeper
Insect muncher
Scaly slitherer
Twirling tongue
Bulging eyes
Drooping chin
Spiked spine
Gripping legs.

Ciara Van Spall (10)
St Andrew's RC Primary School, Streatham

Drought

Drought
No rain,
Dries upland,
Killing plants and people.
Misery.

Daniela Diaz (10)
St Andrew's RC Primary School, Streatham

Working On A Victorian Farm

Leaves scattering everywhere
Birds pecking at the crops.
Birds' wings flapping at tremendous speed
Petrified by the wooden clapper.

Terrified children in the dark freezing cold fields,
One sack to keep them from freezing,
A wooden clapper to scare starving birds away
From the delicious crops.

Sick frightened children, hate having to scare
Terrified starving birds,
Birds and children starving,
But getting nothing to eat.

Sam Dear (9)
St Andrew's RC Primary School, Streatham

The Pulley Workers

The pulley workers are hard-working,
They're always lurking.
They look pretty stressed,
They're really depressed.
They get really sad,
Their jobs are bad.

The pulley workers are freezing cold,
They always say they're going bald.
They sometimes think that they're maids,
They hardly get paid.
They're always lonely,
They walk up, slowly.

Sharna Stephenson (9)
St Andrew's RC Primary School, Streatham

Chimney Sweeps

Chimney sweeps work a long day,
Chimney sweeps work for poor pay.
Chimney sweeps work very hard,
Chimney sweeps work with no card.
Chimney sweeps really sweep away,
Chimney sweeps die where they lay.
Chimney sweeps never have any fun,
Chimney sweeps never ever run,
Chimney sweeps never really sleep,
Chimney sweeps never see any sheep.
Chimney sweeps never have any fun,
Chimney sweeps get shot with a gun.
Bang! Bang! Bang!

Chimney sweeps always get a cold,
Chimney sweeps always eat mould.
Chimney sweeps always have to pay,
Chimney sweeps want to get away.
Chimney sweeps always want to draw,
Chimney sweeps want to obey the law.
Chimney sweeps -
Hate their jobs!

Alexander Warden Feal (9)
St Andrew's RC Primary School, Streatham

The Bird Scarers

In the huge field with damp trees and wet grass,
Your shoes get soaked with water, your backs are bony
And your skin is thin, it's very lonely out there.
We get exhausted and scared with the screeching of birds,
You don't want to scare the birds, because you'll feel very sad.
We don't eat much, we have very skinny bodies.

Daniel Villarosa (9)
St Andrew's RC Primary School, Streatham

The Bird Scarers

The bird scarers, icy and freezing,
The bird scarers, lonely and freezing.
The bird scarers, bored and damp,
The bird scarers, in grassy fields.
The bird scarers, exhausted and gloomy,
The bird scarers, depressed and skinny.
The bird scarers . . .
Don't like their jobs!

The bird scarers, wild winds,
The bird scarers, starving and poor.
The bird scarers, ragged and ripped,
The bird scarers, filthy and messy,
The bird scarers, painfully hurt.
The bird scarers . . .
Want a different job!

Michael McAnea-Hill (9)
St Andrew's RC Primary School, Streatham

Pulley Workers

Pulley workers open and close doors,
While sitting on dusty and dirty floors,
They work all day, no chance to get away,
Staying in the dark all day
All day,
Staying in the dark, all day.

Pulley workers stay up all night,
Sitting there alone with a matter of fright
They have a bad day but they still have to stay,
Walking and watching all day -
All day,
Walking and watching all day.

Claudia Covino (9)
St Andrew's RC Primary School, Streatham

Misery In The Mill

Cotton mill worker, changing bobbins,
Cotton mill worker, working, weeping, weak.
Cotton mill worker, 4p, poor pay,
Cotton mill worker, sore hands all day.
Cotton mill worker, bonnet, ragged clothes,
Cotton mill worker, cleaning machines,
Cotton mill worker, on the weaving loom,
Cotton mill worker, 14 hour shift,
Cotton mill worker, oh so tired!

Emma Johnson (9)
St Andrew's RC Primary School, Streatham

Poverty

Poverty
Sick people,
Starving for food,
Begging for some money,
Imbalance.

Muyiwa Jokotoye (10)
St Andrew's RC Primary School, Streatham

Bird Scarer

I'm a bird scarer, I live alone,
I'm a bird scarer, I have no home.
I'm a bird scarer, eight years of age,
I'm a bird scarer, locked in a cage.

Natasha Nzekwe (9)
St Andrew's RC Primary School, Streatham

Jelly

There is a single type of food
That always puts me in the mood,
And when I find out what's for tea,
I dance around the room with glee!

My favourite is a plate of jelly
Which I spoon into my belly.
But Mummy's always telling me
I can't have jelly for my tea.

Dominic Povall (9)
St Andrew's RC Primary School, Streatham

War

War
Mass destruction,
Murdering human beings,
Evil, hungry for power
Devastation.

Mina Nguyen (10)
St Andrew's RC Primary School, Streatham

Did You Ever See A Lion?

Running machine,
Meat tearer,
Prowling hunter,
Growling roarer,
Furry king!

Andonia Georgio (10)
St Andrew's RC Primary School, Streatham

The Domestic Servants

Life as a servant is
Good and bad.
We like it because
We get a house,
Given orders, makes me
Very sad.
They treat me like a mouse.

I never have time
To sleep, they always
Expect me on my feet.
Most of the time, I have
To leap.
I wish someone could
Give me a treat.

Emma Shepherd (10)
St Andrew's RC Primary School, Streatham

Trappers

I work as a trapper
In a very cold mine,
I am very poor
And I hate opening and closing a door.
I hold a little lamp,
But I also get very cramped.
I feel like a beam
I get hot with lots of steam.

I buy a loaf of bread and some honey,
With my little bit of money.
I also ring a loud heavy bell,
But I feel like hell!

Louis Georgio (9)
St Andrew's RC Primary School, Streatham

Working Children

Heartbroken cold young bodies
Hungry stomachs, muddy feet
Looking at the mean machines, sadly
That's how I'll get to eat.

Complaining about how much they're paid
Only five pence a day,
So tired of being a maid,
'This money's too little.' That's what they say.

Children climbing the long stair
Looking so tired, so sad
Look at their messy hair
Hungry stomachs ache, so bad.

Elizabeth Afon (9)
St Andrew's RC Primary School, Streatham

The Dog And The Horse

The dog and the horse went to Spain
In a nice fast limousine car
They took a large meal and some champagne
And they took it to the bar
The bar
And they took it to the bar.

The horse and the dog flew to Wales
On a speedy plane
The plane went through clouds that left some tails
The clouds then made some rain,
Some rain,
The clouds then made some rain.

Joseph Haddad (9)
St Andrew's RC Primary School, Streatham

Walking To School

On a Wednesday morning,
When I'm still yawning.
I leave the house at twenty-past eight,
To make sure I'm not late.

I run up to the common,
And say good morning to the little old woman
As I pass her by.
With clouds in the sky and birds flying by,
I walk across the damp grass.

At the other end of the park,
I meet Eve and we laugh.
We say, 'Hi!' to the lollipop man,
As he stops a blue van.
Then we both run like hell
Two minutes before the bell.

Ella Felix (9)
St Andrew's RC Primary School, Streatham

Match Day

When I get out of bed
I have toast and egg,
A healthy way
To start my day.

Shirt and shorts and shinpads too,
Don't want to get hurt if someone fouls you,
Ready to play another game,
Come on team, what's our name!

Pass to Joe, flick to Bob,
Well done boys, lovely job.
We're getting closer to the goal,
It's like a big inviting hole.
He aims, he fires, the goalie retires.

Dominic Felix (9)
St Andrew's RC Primary School, Streatham

Chimney Sweepers

Sweep, sweep,
The coal is rushing down the pipe.
Weep, weep,
We're sweeping out all the grime.
Sweep, sweep,
The dust is rushing down the pipe,
Weep, weep,
We're sweeping out one house at a time,
Sweep, sweep,
The soot is rushing down the pipe.
Down the pipe!

Clean, clean,
The dust is floating in the air.
Weep, weep,
When people shout, we just don't care.
Clean, clean,
The soot is floating in the air,
Weep, weep,
The boss walks around in his evil lair.
Clean, clean,
All this dust is in the air,
In the air!

Aimee Fitzsimons (9)
St Andrew's RC Primary School, Streatham

I'm A Little Bulldog

I'm a little bulldog, strong and fast
I'm a bright sun, light and graceful.
I'm a smarty pants, intelligent and quick,
I'm a comfy sofa, comfortable and relaxing.
I'm a cheerful god, funny and fair.

Chaquille Osborne (10)
St Andrew's RC Primary School, Streatham

Me!

I am nervy, like my mum
But she doesn't suck her thumb
Shopping, shopping, that's all we do
Menswear, we haven't got a clue.

My bedroom's pink
And so is my sink
My computer's white
But extremely bright
Swimming is my favourite thing
I am very good and I like to sing.

Dancing comes second
Youth club comes third
But horse riding is the best thing
In the whole, wide world!

Bethany Kirwan-Taylor (9)
St Andrew's RC Primary School, Streatham

Chimney Sweepers

Chimney sweepers stand in the dust
Because we must.
We clean the chimney
Where it's lit very dimly.
We get all dirty and black,
And we never get a snack.

We sweep all day,
And weep all night.
We do it all without a fight.
We do it all until we're so tall,
Then we cannot sweep at all.

Mia Williams (9)
St Andrew's RC Primary School, Streatham

My Car

My car is as fast as a cheetah,
It has as much power as a cheetah
And it roars when it revs up.

My car is warm and soft like a cheetah's tail,
When we are on the motorway all the cars move out of the way
Like we are the fastest animals in the jungle.
My car leaves all the cars in the dust
Like when a cheetah is after its prey.

My car is as slick as a cheetah when it hunts down its prey,
Skidding and darting round to different destinations.
The wheels are like legs when it imprints its paws
Into the jungle mud.
The lights are like the eye of a cheetah
As it targets everything in front of it.
The mouth is like the bonnet of the car,
But watch out for your fingers!
Think of my graceful cheetah,
Think of my dynamic car.

Rhys Perkins Thompson
St Anthony's RC Primary School, Dulwich

Our Car Is A Mother Cat

Smooth like it's just been groomed, the engine starts up
And it gently purrs,
The scent is familiar and comforting,
The tyres pad along the road like a cat's paws,
Despite its largeness, it feels safe,
It is short a bit in length and large a bit in height and width,
The headlamps glow like the eyes of a cat,
Comfortable, safe and warm,
Tyres twist and turn along the road,
The car is a mother cat,
It miaows,
Protecting us as the wind howls.

Jessica O'Donnell (10)
St Anthony's RC Primary School, Dulwich

What Are We?

My muscles are motors
My legs are wheels
The colour of my body is black and tan
My headlights are my eyes.

We both just love speed
We can both change into different gears just like that
We can change our speed to suit our motion or mood
Drive into another gear to prepare for activity
We have the power to do something, we are mentally
                                    and physically strong
We have great energy
We love the contest of speed racing, it is a speciality
We are in control to direct power
We are fast, we act on moving quickly
Quietly, secretly to pursue, persistent to attack or kill
When all is done we make a low vibrant sound expressing pleasure
Then we both smarten ourselves up.

We are a racing car and a cheetah.

Joseph Kelly (10)
St Anthony's RC Primary School, Dulwich

The Worm Tube

The tube was like a fast worm, it needed light to guide it through
                                    the eternal night.
Underground, down deep in the wet soil the train slithers
                                    in endless toil.
Up above where people go, we're moving about but nobody knows.
The rotting smell of oil and smoke makes people want to choke.
The train rattles and clanks along the track,
The worm wriggles in silence to the garden fence and back.

Seamus Wilkinson (9)
St Anthony's RC Primary School, Dulwich

My Journey Through The Vineyards

In the dazzling sun in the south of France,
There I was sitting on a completely open green truck,
Which was just like a toad.

It was an old, clumsy, dry toad,
Scuttling up the vines,
Struggling on each step to go in a straight line.

It was struggling up a steep hill,
Poor wretched thing!
It seemed so thirsty and as sweaty
As an elephant trying to sing.

So there it was, so old, frail and pale,
What a creature! But its painful legs just wouldn't stop,
No matter how much pain it was causing the poor thing.

But my best part of the journey
Was the last hop up onto the top,
Where you could see the whole world
Before your eyes.

Alicia Davies (10)
St Anthony's RC Primary School, Dulwich

Count 1, 2, 3

Count 1, 2, 3
With friends and me.
Bounce, bounce, bounce
Up and down in the playground.

Skip, skip, skip
Skipping with a rope.
Run, run, run
Playing 'it' and having fun.

Donna Webley (6)
St Anthony's RC Primary School, Dulwich

My Pet Puma

My car looks like a blue puma as it races down a hill.
It sounds like a puma as it thunders down the road.
It moves very sleekly and smoothly.
It smells fruity and fresh.
I feel comfortable and as relaxed as an animal sleeping.
It is enormous and wide.

It has headlights for eyes.
The nose is the bonnet.
The mouth is the part under the number plate.
Its ears are the side mirrors.

When it stops my mum puts her foot on the brake slowly
And when it stops completely then the puma stops thundering
And goes to sleep.

Alessandra Boccuzzi (10)
St Anthony's RC Primary School, Dulwich

Is A Seal Like A Boat?

Long and silvery slipping through the water,
Just like a seal the boat dips and speeds in the water
Leaving the land behind,
The seal feeds on fish, but the boat feeds on people.

Like the seal basks on land,
The boat is beached left to dry
While the seal flops and dries basking in the sun,
Soaking up the rays and the seats are dried.

Whilst the seal plays with its pup,
The boat plays with the dinghy it's towing,
Bobbing in the waves like a seal would with its pup,
Rushing in and out of shore.

Are seals and boats alike?

Kate Newby (10)
St Anthony's RC Primary School, Dulwich

The Worm Train

The underground train went through the tunnel
Like a worm sliding through the earth,
The train stopping at the platform
Is like a worm stopping for food.

The train doors are like segments on a worm,
And the mouth of the worm
Reminds me of the train driver's cab.

As the train slowly pulled into the station
I thought about a worm sliding up the garden path,
There was a map of the London underground
And it looked like the paths that a worm takes.

We stopped in a tunnel and the train was quiet
Like the worm underground,
Then the lights went out
And I felt like the worm in the dark soil.

Adam Brady (10)
St Anthony's RC Primary School, Dulwich

Real Animals

A ferry is as big as a whale,
The funnel is like an elephant's trunk,
The ferry moves like an alligator through the water,
The sound of the horn on the funnel goes *honk, honk,*
Like an angry seal.

A helicopter looks like a dragonfly,
The helicopter moves like a bumblebee through the air,
And it sounds like a bumblebee as well,
The sound is like *buzz, buzz,*
Like a butterfly's wings.

Claudia Tua Clark (9)
St Anthony's RC Primary School, Dulwich

Comparing Transport To An Animal!

When I went to France with my family we went on the Eurostar,
I think the Eurostar is like a seal
Because it travels underground and above ground,
The seal is similar because it goes in the sea and on land.

They are similar in other ways like looks and sound,
Also movement and shape.
Seals have long droopy whiskers and large seal eyes
Like the droopy nose of the train,
Both have long and narrow figures that are sleek and smooth.

The Eurostar diving into the tunnel is like a seal sliding into the water.
As the Eurostar chugs into Gard du Nord station
It's like a seal shuffling on some rocks.
When the train is racing through the countryside it is the best bit,
It's like a seal skimming through water.
When the driver honks the horn it's like a seal barking.

Elizabeth Crilly (9)
St Anthony's RC Primary School, Dulwich

The Duck

A ferry is like a duck,
Gliding along the water,
Cruising on the sea,
Oh look what I can see.

The ferry is moving fast,
As smoothly as can be,
The surfer glistening upon the ocean,
Travellers putting on suntan lotion.

The ferry is coming closer,
Nearing to its end,
The duck is following on,
Both turning round the bend.

Kiefer Rodrigues (10)
St Anthony's RC Primary School, Dulwich

Animal Transport

On a slightly windy but warm evening, there are many colourful
hot air balloons in the sky:
A few moments later the hot air balloons transform
into rather huge, round, plump pigs.
They squeal and squirm to be free and trot towards the sunset.

Below the pig, we have the tube,
It looks exactly like a long, colourless worm tunnelling
through the ground,
She moves around blindly, seeking a place to rest after a long day.

Early in the morning the car is in his den,
A jaguar, prince of the jungle, ready to pounce on his pitiful prey,
He rumbles with hunger and his headlights are wide open searching,
His long, silky tail sways to the side as he waits.

In the sky, there is an eagle,
A huge towering metal eagle,
Her powerful wings beat against the clouds,
The windows are the eyes searching for a place to land,
She screeches loudly as she sees another bird.

Far out to sea, the ferry is riding the waters,
She is just like an enormous whale,
She splashes along happily with steam rising out from her blowhole,
And she leaves behind a trail of foam bubbling sluggishly as she goes.

Dai-Khue Le-Duong (10)
St Anthony's RC Primary School, Dulwich

The Train

The train traverses the mountain.
Round and round it snakes around.
Into a tunnel, up a hill,
This colourful snake will speedily thrill.
Chugging through the city
Like a pouncing grass snake.

Luisa Boselli Alcock (10)
St Anthony's RC Primary School, Dulwich

My Poem About Boreatton Park

Boreatton Park here we come, ready for loads of fun.
Wet or dry we don't care, as long as all my friends are there.
On the river we canoe with Mrs Duddy, Fia too.
A paddle for me and a paddle for you,
going backwards, what do we do?
Paddle along we sang a song,
we must be good we scared a swan.
Mrs Casey was wicked and came for a laugh,
at the end of the day we all needed a bath.
Mr Vernazza got involved and being so cool
just the same as if at school.
Mr Closkey was funny and ever so mad,
making everyone happy not sad.
Now time for bed, get ready for home,
Boreatton Park we will now leave you alone.

Adele Jakeman (10)
St Joseph's RC School, Hanwell

Abseiling

Abseiling
You have to
Lean back
Into thin air
Which gives you a little bit of a scare.

When you look down
From up so high
You think, *will I make it*
Will I survive?

Nearly there
Now almost done
A smile on my face
What great fun!

Connor O'Brien (10)
St Joseph's RC School, Hanwell

The Ape

There was an ape who liked to beg,
He begged from the president and lost his legs.
There was an ape who stole from a farm,
Got hit by a cow and lost his arm.
There was an ape who stole a bed,
Got hit by a pillow and lost his head.
And when he thought he lost all his body parts,
He fell on a rock and lost his heart.
He is a king and thinks he's the best,
Got hit by a bag and lost his biceps.
He is very dumb, he uses words like uh and duh.
His friend got so angry and accidentally committed murder.
Finally he tried to think of one body part he hadn't lost,
Just one, then when he sat down he lost his bum.

Thomas Dawood (10)
St Joseph's RC School, Hanwell

Raft Building

Raft building, raft building
What great fun
Put it in the water
All jump on.

Raft building, raft building
What great fun
Too many children
Can they all swim?

Raft building, raft building
What great fun
Someone leans over the edge
We all fall in.

Splash!

Jeremy Hunt (10)
St Joseph's RC School, Hanwell

Dog's Park

I drove to Dog's Park
While it was still dark
I had to be up with the lark
Because of my dog's bark.

When we got there
Sparky and Sharky enjoyed the space,
They ran wild and free
Chasing the birds and squirrels
Up into the trees.

Then we went home
They were happy and contented
I gave them a drink
They went to their shed
And I went to my bed.

It was time for me
You see
To catch up on my sleep
Under my fleece.

Idran John T Algozo (10)
St Joseph's RC School, Hanwell

Zip Wire

Zip wire, zip wire is high and fast,
Down you go with a blast.

The wind feels good in your face,
Your heart is filled with fun and grace.

The noise it makes,
Is like a snake.

Sylvia Oleniacz (10)
St Joseph's RC School, Hanwell

Boreatton Park

I went to Boreatton Park
And I didn't even notice when it got dark
No one was lazy
But some people were crazy.

On the zip wire I was so scared
But no one seemed to care
The abseiling was good
Better than the food.

It was very cool
At least away from school
Instead of sitting in class
I was playing on the grass.

The days went quickly
I didn't want to go
But I felt I should
Get home before the snow.

Anna Winnicka (10)
St Joseph's RC School, Hanwell

Abseiling

Abseiling, abseiling
Over the top,
Step by step,
Make sure you don't drop.
Abseiling, abseiling
What fantastic fun,
The ropes hold you up,
So you don't hurt your bum.
Abseiling, abseiling
You've reached the floor,
Up the ladder you go
To do some more.

George Oller (10)
St Joseph's RC School, Hanwell

There Was A Dog

There was a dog
Who went to fetch a log
And then he ran after a hog.

He was quite mental
But sometimes gentle,
He ate his waste and liked the taste.

His owner was also mad
And thought his dog was bad.
He threw his dog out into the street
With nothing to eat,
And that was the end of a dog
Called Little Bow Peat.

Vanessa Dawod (11)
St Joseph's RC School, Hanwell

Zip Wire

Zip wire, zip wire, oh my zip wire
I would love to ride on you zip wire.

Zip wire, zip wire, you're going too fast,
I can see everything
And smell the fresh air.

Zip wire, I can hear something,
It's the zzz sound in the air.

Oh zip wire, zip wire, it's time to go,
I enjoyed riding on you zip wire,
I would love to ride in you again
And again and again . . .

Tyrene Daoey (11)
St Joseph's RC School, Hanwell

Naughty Dog

A dog ran barking out of his garden
To escape from having his bath.

His master was too slow for him
That's why he couldn't catch him.

He ran to the park barking
He scratched a car and a man jumped out.

The man was running after him
Luckily the dog jumped and the man smashed into the wall
His master said, 'Where were you? You need your bath.'
And the dog fell down.

Karlo Filipczak (11)
St Joseph's RC School, Hanwell

Buddy

So small he could sleep in a welly
Faster than a blink of an eye
Four tiny legs, an inquisitive nose
So, so busy, so many places to go

His brown, velvety coat, so soft
Ears that don't miss a sound
Eyes that sparkle with mischief
There's no peace when Buddy's around

As last, all quiet and peaceful
Buddy's asleep in his bed
Faint snores echo softly
As puppy dreams dance in his head.

Christine O'Rourke (10)
St Joseph's RC School, Hanwell

The Cat In The Hat

There was once a cat in a hat
Now fancy that
A cat in a hat
This cat liked to sing
Because he thought he was a king
He took his hat off
To find a golden moth
He jumped for joy
And hit a boy on his way to his house
Cat bashed down the door
Finding he had broken the law
Then finding a boy and girl
The cat began to twirl
The girl and boy
Called Conrad and Sally
Helped Cat up
Sally asked
'Cat, can you make cupcakes?'
'Yes I can, out of anything.'
So they put in some plates
Into the cupcake maker
They started all looking
To find the cakes were cooking
Cat took out the cakes
And put them onto plates
Meaning Conrad, Sally and Cat
Were all good mates.

Dominic Campbell (10)
St Joseph's RC School, Hanwell

Kitten

So small kitten as a ball of fur,
Running down my garden fence,
Cuddles in my arms with no sense,
Bed I say,
I lay,
Him in his warm bed,
Dreaming in his head.

The next day,
He wakes me up with his smooth tongue,
Licking my face.

Then he jumps off my bed,
And he stands in the middle of the room,
Miaowing to hug him,
So I do!

Veronika Lukomska (10)
St Joseph's RC School, Hanwell

Archery

Archery, archery
What great *fun*
Don't do star jumps
When one man
Got his bow and arrow
Trying to shoot you.

Archery, archery
What great fun
It was too late
The man shot
Five arrows at the boy.

Kevin Kailani (10)
St Joseph's RC School, Hanwell

The Fox And The Dog

The fox and the dog
were two best friends
they would always play with each other
and their friendship never ended.
They were supposed to be enemies
said the others
but they loved each other
like they were brothers.
As the days went by
they grew older and older
but their friendship grew stronger
and nights went colder.
They grew up together
the fox and the dog
now they go to Heaven together
awaiting God.

Rohaid Joseph (11)
St Joseph's RC School, Hanwell

Abseiling

When I climbed to the top of the tower
It looked as if I had just climbed to the top of Mount Everest
I was so scared when I looked down
It was as if I was going to fall off.

It felt as if my heart was going to stop beating,
As if my heart was going to sink into my stomach,
As if my heart was going to explode.

As soon as I started to walk down the tower
I thought it was so bad I became so sad
My mates started to say, 'Jay, you're good,
At least you're not bad.'

Jay James (10)
St Joseph's RC School, Hanwell

The Running Mustang

A mustang was running through the cold night of the desert
He was cold like ice, he was desperate to have a drink
He ran and ran and ran and ran but he heard something, 'Woohoo.'
Wolves surrounded him in a circle and said, 'Let us kill you.'
Their mouths were bloody, the mustang started to run.
He jumped over the wolves, the wolves started to run after him.
They nearly caught him but he fell into the water.
The wolves were petrified of the water,
The mustang started to splash the water at the wolves
And they all ran away.
He saw some lights, he ran into the village where he was loved
And cared for.

Aleksander Filipczak (11)
St Joseph's RC School, Hanwell

Cheeky Monkey

The cheeky monkey climbs up the tree
To grab all the bananas that he can see
He sits and stares
Maybe he wishes they were pears

Brothers and sister join for a while
From the treetop they can see for a mile
Peeling and eating their favourite lunch
They all seem to be a well-fed bunch

Playing, swinging and messing about
The cheeky monkey lets out a shout
They hurry on down a little unsure
Knowing that they could have had more

The cheeky monkey climbs down the tree
To check on the other three
He sees them in a tree nearby
And wishes he could fly.

Michael Huguenin (10)
St Joseph's RC School, Hanwell

Jacob's Ladder

Boreatton Park here we come,
we're gonna have loads of fun.
No one told us it would test our courage,
till they showed us Jacob's Ladder.
We all shouted, 'We're not playing,'
but then they taught us bee laying.
V to the knee 1, 2, 3,
to get ourselves up we had to climb.
I couldn't have done it without my friends,
I used their knees to climb with ease.

We climbed and climbed to our hearts' content,
we stood at the top
and felt the wind flow through our bodies.
We yelled, 'We've done it!'
We were so proud.
We jumped from log to log
as they pulled us down.

Ciara Ash (10)
St Joseph's RC School, Hanwell

Mother

God chose you from the rest,
because you know you are the best.

He gave you a lion heart,
and still you never let me down.

Your qualities are one in all,
so I was sent like a baby so small.

You guide me through my life along,
God knew I needed someone strong.

So he chose you from all the rest,
he was right, you are the best.

Prosper Ezewuzie (10)
St Joseph's RC School, Hanwell

Boreatton Park

Boreatton Park here we come
we are ready for loads of fun!
We are ready for all the fantastic activities that come along
swinging across zip wire, climbing Jacob's Ladder
and canoeing along the river all day long.
We are ready to walk down the abseiling tower
because we are full of loads of power.

Our groupies are coming to meet us
and play lots of fantastic games with us.
It is going to be a special week full of loads of breaks.
My cabin is great with all my mates
who are a pleasure to be with.
Teachers coming in at every hour
complaining about the noise
because we are jumping up with joy.
We sing loads of songs,
long ones and short ones.

Oh what a brilliant week it has been!

Fia-Louise Shannon Lane (10)
St Joseph's RC School, Hanwell

Boreatton Park: Raft Building

The night before I couldn't sleep
how would we get on this week?
Would we all miss our mums?
Yahoo! Raft building here we come
The instructor taught us while we listened
to build a raft with skill and craft
Barrels, rope and log, helped us do the job
On the raft we laughed and laughed
as we sailed down the river
Even people falling in didn't mind the shiver
but the cold went all the way to their liver.

Richard Nolan (10)
St Joseph's RC School, Hanwell

Stallion

The ice-white stallion gallops through the dark forest
as the moonlight glitters in her eyes,
not aware of the wolves following her scent.
The crack of twigs underneath,
as she turns she meets the wolves' gaze as they slowly circle her.

No one could help her at this time of night,
but as the time passes, clocks tick.
The wolves get nearer by the second,
her dark brown eyes fill with tears, no one can help her.

Bloodthirsty jaws opening wide
with saliva dribbling from their mouths.
As they target their prey, how will she survive this winter's night?
As her thoughts are turned into actions,
she hurtles forward over the snarling and vicious wolves,
back once more into the dark forest.

Hannah Banks (10)
St Joseph's RC School, Hanwell

Boreatton Park - The Climbing Wall

The climbing wall was alarmingly high,
it poked through the light blue sky.
I climbed the wall while the clouds passed by,
I thought I was about to fly.

The top of the tower was very tall,
but the people down below were very small.
'Jump down quickly,' they called,
round and down I jumped and had a fall.

I reached the bottom with a big thud,
on the ground I firmly stood.
My feet were squelching in the mud,
I smiled, it felt so good.

Alessandro De Rose (10)
St Joseph's RC School, Hanwell

The Haunted Castle

In a castle dark and musty,
Stood a suit of armour ever so rusty.
Haunted from plate to visor,
People were none the wiser.

Then one day the suit went walking by,
Passed some people who were talking,
All they could do was stand there gawping.

'Run!' the guide said
And soon everyone had fled.
The ghostly suit marched down the hall,
Shut the door and frightened them all.

At night it used its ghostly powers
To howl from the castle towers.
It clinked and clinked and stomped around,
And made a wailing and creaking sound.

Soon the news spread far and wide,
And queues of people lined outside,
A great big crowd had come to see
The spooky ghost that wandered free.

He meant to scare them all away,
So he left that very day!

Samsara Bachoo (10)
St Joseph's RC School, Hanwell

Free At Last

The charming horse gallops in the green hills,
She is happy to be free at last,
Her mane flows freely in the wind,
As her hooves hit the fresh ground at last,
Just the same as it was in the past.

Olivia Edwards (10)
St Joseph's RC School, Hanwell

My First School Journey

On Monday morning we boarded a coach,
We talked and we laughed and told lots of jokes.
Half-past four, hip hip hooray,
We're at Boreatton Park, what a tiring day.

It's Tuesday morning and there's lots in store,
Zip wire, abseiling and much, much more.

After dinner it's time to talk,
Then back to our cabin, it's not a long walk.

On Wednesday morning we had a lie-in,
Canoeing was great until we fell in.
Jacob's Ladder was hard but of course so brill,
We had a disco that night and dressed to kill

It's Thursday already, I can't believe it's our last day,
Some more activities are coming my way.
Our last evening has arrived and I must say,
The 'have-a-go show' was laughs all the way.

On Friday morning before our departure,
We built a raft, what a disaster.
It's time to go home and rejoin my family,
But I'll never forget my first school journey.

Alana Pearson (10)
St Joseph's RC School, Hanwell

Manchester United

M an U are the best you got to admit
A rsenal have no chance in the Premiership
N ow Chelsea and Man U don't mix
U nited have the ability and the tricks
N ow all the players are really good
I t would be great to play for them, it should
T ell me are Man U the best?
E very player
D eserves to have a rest.

Fadi Mansour
St Joseph's RC School, Hanwell

Boreatton Park

Boreatton Park food was nice,
We had burgers, chips and rice.
It was really nice.
The puddings were great,
We ate and ate lots of chocolate cake.

During the day at Boreatton Park,
We had lots and lots of fun.
We did an assault course, zip wire,
Rock climbing, raft building,
And lots, lots more.
It was brilliant.

I fell in the water,
I thought I was going to lose my life,
But along came Jenny and saved my life.

At night at Boreatton Park,
I shared a cabin with mates.
We stayed up really late,
Last but not least we had a midnight feast.

Jamie Brady (10)
St Joseph's RC School, Hanwell

Flowers!

Roses are red, violets are blue,
Tulips are pink although they do stink.

Roses are red, violets are blue,
Daffodils are yellow, that's why we say hello.

Roses are red, violets are blue,
Lilies are white, at least they don't bite.

Roses are red, violets are blue,
Bluebells are blue, that's why I chose you!

Tracy Wahome (10)
St Joseph's RC School, Hanwell

Jacob's Ladder Experience

The teachers walked me to Jacob's Ladder as nerves ran through me,
I shivered inside with coldness flowing round me.
I saw the logs we had to climb, some were worried, some were elated,
but I was fine. I had determination as the instructor put the harness on.
I chose my companions and it made me excited.

We were first to go up, up to the top was my goal,
nothing could stop me, it was amazing to know.
On the first ladder we stepped, ready to face the moment of truth.
Climb on, climb on to the fourth one, three more to go.
Friends were crying, I tried to help but they got down.
Only two to climb, not three, oh what a pity, we did our best.

The two girls pushed themselves up to the top.
We were so pleased, even though we used all our ease.
Jumping down like abseiling from log to log, we were on the ground.

My heart fell down to my knees, even though I was so pleased.
Hip hip hooray, I did Jacob's Ladder today.
Got to go now, back to our cabins. Bye!

Emily Barker (10)
St Joseph's RC School, Hanwell

Boreatton Park

It was funny and happy
It was wet and rainy
It was hard work
But it was worth it
I came back happy but tired.

Activities were hard to do
We did jumps
And mucked around
It was tough but so much fun.

Activities were funny and happy
I did them with big pleasure.

David Kupis (11)
St Joseph's RC School, Hanwell

My Poem About Love

You're so beautiful, you're so smart,
To me you're a work of art.
A winter coat for billy goat,
Or underwear for a grizzly bear.
Soft white gloves for turtle doves,
Or a pair of socks for a smart red fox.

Ashlee Tailapathy (10)
St Joseph's RC School, Hanwell

The Hurricane Season

The morning was bright,
The sun was right,
The day looked like a perfect treat,
It was a surprise, a hurricane brought a defeat,
It moaned, groaned, whirled, swirled and the weather never got better.

Danielle Isaac-Simon (11)
St Joseph's RC School, Hanwell

Friends

My friend has hair that looks like a bear
And my friend is tall, he plays basketball.
He is shy, he has a tie.
He is tall, he hit a wall and he is huge.
He can touch everything.
My friend is cool, he is not short.
My friend is cool, he's better than anyone
And he is so, so, so big, he can touch the sky.
He is tall, he can swim and is so tall
He can eat lots.

Laura Joseph (6)
St Joseph's RC Primary School, Willesden

God's Creation

In the beginning God created Heaven and Earth.
He made the sun, the moon and stars.
God made the snow, he made day and night.
He made the wonderful clouds.
God made a man and woman
And told them to look after the animals.
God made thunder and lightning.
He made the people walk and talk.
He made the trees and bees.
God created the day and night.
He helps me to run and have fun.
God made winter and wind.
He made you and me.

Jennáé Cox (7)
St Joseph's RC Primary School, Willesden

Friends

My friend has a tie, he is shy.
My big brother is tall, he plays basketball.
I ride a bike, I like it like Mike.
My friend is clever for ever.
My dad cries and eats fries.
My mum is short, she can play sport.
I look and read interesting books.
My friend eats a pear like a bear.
An ant is on the floor, he can't reach the door.
My brother is silly like Billy.
My friend is poor, he always says, 'Roar!'

Ricky German (6)
St Joseph's RC Primary School, Willesden

Our World

God created the day,
God created the month called May.
He made us run,
He made us have lots of fun.
He created the light,
Even the night.
God created the trees,
Even the bumblebees.
God created the moon and the sun,
He even created lots of fun.
God is great and good,
Let us thank Him for our food.
God created us,
He even made everyone fuss.

Adam Soerjowidjojo (8)
St Joseph's RC Primary School, Willesden

The Mysterious Dog

I see a dog
Chasing a cat.
It is running,
It is brown.
Its fur is very smooth.
Its body is square
With a round face.
It barks at suspicious people.
It can dance.
He likes licking people and he is helpful.

Chloe Bofukia & Catherine Anteson
St Joseph's RC Primary School, Willesden

Friends

I help my friends when they are on the floor,
And I am going to play with my friends.
I am going to care for my friend.
I am going to share with my new good friend.
I will like my new good friend.
I will take my new friend to the teacher when they are hurt.
I won't hurt my friend. I will play nice with my friends.

Oliver Beckford (6)
St Joseph's RC Primary School, Willesden

Cat

I see a cat
Nice and fat.
It moves very slow
And it likes sitting on a mat.
It likes jumping walls
And likes the fish that swim.
He doesn't get wet because he's the best pet.

Shauneil Tavernier-Antoine (8)
St Joseph's RC Primary School, Willesden

I See A Dog

I see a dog
It is rolling around.
It jumps like a flea.
Its colour is black.
It makes a noise
Like this: *bark, bark.*
It scratches its ear
When itchy.

Marcel Ramlal (8)
St Joseph's RC Primary School, Willesden

The Bad Cat

I see a bad cat chasing a mouse around the back garden.
It is roaring with anger.
It is ginger with big blue marble eyes.
The cat is rather slim and rather fat.
Its fur looks soft and gentle, but also a bit spiky.
It makes a miaowy sound.
It lays around all day.
Also it eats quite a lot.

Lara Williams (8)
St Joseph's RC Primary School, Willesden

Cool Cat

I see a cat,
Waiting to pounce,
Sneaking around the room,
Its colour is black,
It is round and fat,
Its skin is soft like its fur,
Miaow and purr!
It will sit on your lap,
I love my cat.

Georgie Roche-Low (8)
St Joseph's RC Primary School, Willesden

School Life

School is sometimes fun,
at playtime kids like to run.
Detentions are really bad,
the teachers hate children who are mad.
The children in school have to walk,
they always like to talk.
At lunchtime it's really loud,
in class kids' heads are up in the cloud.

Joel Soerjowidjojo (10)
St Joseph's RC Primary School, Willesden

God's Creation

God created the land,
and all the sand.
God created the fish.
Our Lord created the sun,
the moon and the stars.
Our Lord created the creatures of the sea,
the mountains, the jungles.

God created boys and girls
God created men and women
God created plants and trees,
God created rivers, streets
and God created shops.

God gave me a heart,
He gave me a smile,
I thank You because You made me a child.

God, I love You for all the things You have made
around me and in other countries.

Kerri O'Toole (8)
St Joseph's RC Primary School, Willesden

Hands

Your hands are useful for lots of things,
they are much, much better than fairies' wings.
Without them you won't get a hug,
or pick up slimy little slugs.

On my fingertips are nails,
when they are clean they are very pale.
Pretty patterns I paint on,
but when it's time for school they must be gone,
and often with my palms I can walk along.

Lauren Emsden (9)
St Joseph's RC Primary School, Willesden

God's Beautiful Creation

God made the land,
it was just like the sand.
He created all the creatures
that live in the sea.

God made the stars
but He didn't make the cars.
God created boys and girls
and men and women.

God likes to make people happy.
He likes to put smiles on your faces.
God made all the beautiful places.

I thank You Lord for Your beautiful world,
We all thank You very much,
And I thank You for my hands so I can touch.

Hayley Hill (8)
St Joseph's RC Primary School, Willesden

The Slithering Snake

I see a snake,
Going through the grass,
Slithering and creeping like a panther
Ready to pounce.
It is brown but in camouflage,
Long and round.
Its skin is flaky and scaly,
It makes a hissing sound.
It sheds its skin,
Tongue as sharp as a pin,
And going for its prey.

Michael Freduah-Appouh (8)
St Joseph's RC Primary School, Willesden

Dove

Don't you just love
Little doves?
They fly around,
They don't make a sound,
Oh, they do when they're singing,
Like a bell ringing.
They are white,
They shine in the night.
They give you a rose,
They kiss your nose.
They are like rice,
But they're really nice.
Everyone loves
Doves!

Klaudia Staniszewska (9)
St Joseph's RC Primary School, Willesden

Barr Barr

I see a parrot,
Tweet, tweet, tweet,
Stealing crackers,
Copying what you say,
Steals it off you, you cry.
Thieving jewels
From caves of Wonderland.
Do not get jacked
So beware of the parrot,
The skateboard parrot rider.

Jean-Luc Mutesa (8)
St Joseph's RC Primary School, Willesden

My Friend

My friend Derek is nice,
he likes to eat rice.

His favourite colour is red,
he spends all the time in bed.

He liked a book,
he forgot to look.

He lost his dad,
he played with Chad.

He likes to run,
but he never has fun.

He has a cat,
he always wears his hat.

He doesn't like rats,
but they sit on his mats.

Matthew Halpin (6)
St Joseph's RC Primary School, Willesden

I See A Loving Dog

I see a loving dog chasing a cat,
Running slow like she's fat.
The colour of her skin is white and black.
She's shaped like a sausage-shaped bat.
She's smooth and fluffy just like a cat.
She growls when she's angry.
She hunts for birds very badly.
She likes it when you stroke her
And she smiles gladly.

Chanelle St Louis (8)
St Joseph's RC Primary School, Willesden

My Friend

My friend Matthew is fun, better than anyone.
He is scared of mice, he thinks they're not very nice.
He likes to read books, he doesn't make me look.
He is the best, better than the rest.
He likes to play a lot, then draws with dot to dot.
He likes to go to the library, but only takes the books out for free.
He likes to come to my house to look at my mouse.
He has a cat that wears a hat.
He is nice and likes to eat rice.
He is good like he should be.
He plays with balls and kicks them on the wall.
He is really neat and is very sweet.

Tori Drummond (6)
St Joseph's RC Primary School, Willesden

Graceful

I see a horse gracefully gliding
Its hair in the sun and breeze
It is gliding its hooves in the race
Hopefully winning
It is the colour brown and gold
It is neighing
Looking down on the grass
Graceful horses
I want you.

Sheila (8)
St Joseph's RC Primary School, Willesden

My Friends

My friend is Tori, she is the best
She is better than the rest
She is always telling jokes that are funny
She likes blue because she is stuck to glue
She likes school and goes to the swimming pool
Tori is sweet because she is neat
She has a cat who sits on a mat
She has a dog who sits on a log
She has a rat who sleeps on a hat
She has a cat who has a hat
She has a rat who sits on a bat
She has a dog who sits on a bug
She has a frog who sits on a bog.

Aine Mackin (6)
St Joseph's RC Primary School, Willesden

Mouse Catcher

My cat is a bird hunter,
He makes his tail twitch and is a whisker bristler.
He pounces and bounces.
He was leaping and sleeping,
My cat is a bed nicker,
Ball toyer and a fish taker.
His name is Mark and he is afraid of the dark.
Mark barks and he makes a noise - *purr!*

Tayla Humphris (8)
St Joseph's RC Primary School, Willesden

My Friend

My friend Kevin plays games with silly names.
He is nice but he likes to eat rice.
He likes to run because he is fun.
He is a boy, I give him joy.
He is good as he should be.
He is the best, better than the rest.
He is so sweet, but he is neat.
His favourite colour is green, he doesn't want to clean.
He wants to read a book and he likes to cook.
He comes to my house to see my little mouse.

Derek Ariho (6)
St Joseph's RC Primary School, Willesden

Movements

Dingoes chase,
Horses race.

Mice creep,
Cats sneak.

Bulls charge,
Elephants barge.

Young animals have fun,
But -
I run!

Alexandra Ferrari (8)
St Joseph's RC Primary School, Willesden

My Friend

My friend is Reuben, he plays games, he likes silly names.
He is the best, better than the rest.
He is always fun, he likes to run.
He is a boy, I give him joy.
He is so sweet, but he is neat.
He likes to come to my house to see my mouse.
He has a cat who sits on a mat.
He is a boy, he shares his toy.
He is good, he has a hood.

Kevin Valencia (6)
St Joseph's RC Primary School, Willesden

The Greedy Mouse

There was a mouse
that lived in someone's house.
It was so stout,
It was a like a tomcat.

It crept slowly
in a low prowl.
The mouse had a little home
in the house.

It squeaked lowly
in a low sound.
He was so greedy.
He always ate cheese.

Nathan Nwaokolo (8)
St Joseph's RC Primary School, Willesden

World War II

Bombs are exploding all around me,
Boats and tanks are all I can see.

People hiding, it's all in a bad state,
When people are dying, you wonder where's your mate.

It's hard to remember, that's all I can say,
Oh yeah! Now I remember, I hope I live today.

Now I am trying not to die,
Whatever I say, it won't be a lie.

I am someone who works as a nurse,
'Oh my goodness, I've lost my purse!'
Hitler's bad,
He's made people sad.

Whenever you lay,
Always remember you have to pray.

Luke McLean
St Joseph's RC Primary School, Willesden

World War II

It is time for me to go to war.
Please God help me through this terrible roar.
People dying and turning into dust.
Blood pouring out of the glass and rust.
The RAF flying high.
Children looking up in the sky.
People dying every day and night.
People full of fright at the sights.
Children being evacuated every day and night.
Guns blazing everywhere.
War is over so let's say 'Hooray' and fly home today.

James Meredith
St Joseph's RC Primary School, Willesden

World War II

Many people will be killed,
So much blood will be spilled,
Children are evacuated,
The sirens are ringing,
Air raid alert,
Get to your bomb shelter,
Get your gas mask or be killed,
There are many injured soldiers,
Many of them have died for our country,
The planes are fighting,
Who will win?
The boats and tanks are coming to defend,
We can't lose, now let's fight,
Germany's planes are hitting the ground
Can we win?
The Arian race is coming,
Get the weapons, we ain't losing this war
Himmler sends the secret service
Get in the tanks, the planes, the boats
And defend with our lives.

Fintan Curley (10)
St Joseph's RC Primary School, Willesden

All About Cats

Cats' shiny eyes,
The soft fur from cats,
Mice eaters,
Hunters for birds,
Greedy for fish,
Sharp whiskers,
Tail whippers,
Gate climbers,
Ear spikers.

Shyheim Brown Orlebar (8)
St Joseph's RC Primary School, Willesden

World War II

While bombs are pounding,
And planes are in the skies,
The sirens are sounding,
See the fear in Hitler's eyes.

Men are marching round with guns,
While Hitler's getting cross,
The tanks that weigh some tonnes,
Have made the world war loss.

Children are getting scared,
As Hitler is the boss,
Everything is always shared,
But Hitler then lost.

Niamh Fitzpatrick (10)
St Joseph's RC Primary School, Willesden

Adolf Hitler

I am the leader of Germany,
No one is stronger than me.

I am strong and powerful,
Everybody's scared of me
Because I'm big and sourful.

No man is more powerful than me,
No man in history.

Poland, England, Scotland, Wales,
They are all scared of me
So they hide under train rails.

So, don't get near me,
Or if you do you'll see!

Adrianna Pawelec
St Joseph's RC Primary School, Willesden

Our World - God's Creation

God made the moon
n the night, so soon.
God made the moon for night,
God made the sun for it will be bright.

God made the world,
He made the fish,
they swim in the sea,
and you can see bees.
God made our mouths to talk,
and our legs to walk.
He brings us light,
and the lovely time of night.

Oh, the lovely joy He brings,
it gives us the joy to sing,
God brought us here,
sometimes we have tears,
but every single one of us will grow up with happy smiles,
and we will have dreams for miles and miles and miles,
until it comes to an end.

Acayo Okello (7)
St Joseph's RC Primary School, Willesden

My Primary School

I go to school every day
My teacher earns her pay
She tells me off, if I'm in trouble
She pounces on me on the double
She is really nice
Like soft boiled rice
I wouldn't change her for the world
As she is as good as gold.

Steven McDonnell (10)
St Joseph's RC Primary School, Willesden

Our World

God created the stars,
God let us have cars.

God made us smile,
While our mum was walking down the aisle.

God made me stay alive,
When I was stuck in a beehive.

God let us have fun,
He was able to make me run.

God made us so we could walk,
God was able to let us talk.

God gave us bones,
God made the stones.

He made our mums give birth,
The Lord made us all on Earth.

God made the sun and sea,
God loves me.

Chanel German (7)
St Joseph's RC Primary School, Willesden

Sneaky Cat

I see a sneaky cat,
Who eats like a bat.
Slowly pouncing,
And quickly leaping,
Cunning cat enjoys sleeping.
I see a sneaky cat,
Who is just far too fat
That it hardly moves
A single inch,
With paws like horses' hooves.

Amanda Amoah (8)
St Joseph's RC Primary School, Willesden

The Black Cat

She is a young creature
with a sleek black coat,
and prowls round all night,
under her warm plush cloak.

She catches her prey
and on her way
she goes off into the night.

She stops to look
at the road she took
and disappears into the night.

She is a young creature
with a sleek plush coat,
she is shy and obliged to go on,
but she will not stop
until the time comes
to be out of the night and gone.

Isabella Lau (9)
St Mary's School, Hampstead

Do Oysters Sneeze?

Do oysters sneeze beneath the seas,
Or wiggle to and fro,
Or sulk or smile or dance awhile,
How can we ever know?

Do oysters yawn when roasted at dawn,
And do they ever weep?
And can you tell when in its shell
An oyster is asleep?

Veronica Cappelli (9)
St Mary's School, Hampstead

The Racehorse

The racehorse
is ready
to race the course,
the huffs and the puffs
from the horses ready to race.

I'm on one
ready to race
to go with the pace.

I'm ready, steady, *go!*
The horses run
as if it's fun,
it is not,
it's scary and hot.

I hear my name, Mary,
we jump a jump,
my heart starts to pump.

I'm first, second, third,
I hear a bird go tweet, tweet,
a rush of air,
a blow of wind,
I'm off, I jump, I fall
I'm *dead!*

Katie Dillon (9)
St Mary's School, Hampstead

Puss!

It can prowl and sprowl,
It miaows, it's not a cow.
It's got whiskers, I always kiss her,
She eats biscuits, the company's called Whiskets.
She has a white bit and four creamy socks,
She sometimes has a kip when she starts to doze off.

Mia Yates (9)
St Mary's School, Hampstead

Dogs

Dogs, dogs raining everywhere
like to chase certain animals
such as the flashing hare.
A glorious day to have a play
with your lovely, cuddly dog.
Humph . . . he has his way.
Dogs, dogs raining everywhere,
Look, there's a guard dog
and she has the dog mayor!
Dogs are fun,
dogs are cute
look, even my friend has one.
Fluffy, soft collie,
belonging to Suzy Molly.
Dogs can be . . . giant
they can be clients.
   Dogs are lovely,
   dogs are bubbly,
   dogs, dogs raining everywhere,
   when you need a hand dogs are . . .
      there!

Natasha Rosas (9)
St Mary's School, Hampstead

Leopard

The day is too hot,
The night is too cold,
The king of Africa,
The one that's so bold,
Seen its prey,
Ready to pounce,
Creeping up closer . . .
Pounce!

Aoife Casson (9)
St Mary's School, Hampstead

A Swan

S erene
W hite
A ttractive
N oble

There it sits in the sunset
Grooming its feathers now and then
On the blazing lake it sleeps
Never making a sound or beep
It paddles and swims to and fro
Showing off like a person on stage.

When it goes on land
Can't stop chasing you until there's a stroke of a hand.

Akanksha Gupta (9)
St Mary's School, Hampstead

The Elephant

Elephant, elephant
eats the grass
Elephant, elephant
don't look in the looking glass
Elephant, elephant
is not like a giraffe
Elephant, elephant
breaks the bricks
Elephant, elephant
eats Weetabix
Elephant, elephant
looks after six
Elephant, elephant
goes to bed with pick 'n' mix.

Amelia Gelson-Thomas (9)
St Mary's School, Hampstead

The Cheating Cheetah

Cheetah, cheetah climb the wall
Cheetah, cheetah eat the ball
Cheetah, cheetah make new friends
Cheetah, cheetah our love never ends

Cheetah, cheetah prowl around
Cheetah, cheetah bound up and down
Cheetah, cheetah look in the ball
Cheetah, cheetah take a call
Cheetah, cheetah fall off the wall
Cheetah, cheetah broke his neck
Cheetah, cheetah turned into Shrek.

Shrek had a pointy nose
And don't forget his toes
Shrek had a nice life
With his ogre sized wife.

Saoirse Cussen (9)
St Mary's School, Hampstead

Who Am I?

I am green like the grass
Yet also dirty brass

Part of me falls off one time of the year
I have no legs nor mouth, not an ear

I am rough on the outside but not within
I am ever so quiet you could hear a pin

I stay sometimes from here to there
I have no house, not a carpet, nor chair

I think you should know now that you see
I am absolutely most definitely a tree!

Ailish Maroof (9)
St Mary's School, Hampstead

Monkeys

His coat of fur is draping across the ground,
Suddenly he springs up, his tail winding around him.
There is a big screech in the air, he is petrified, frozen you could say.
His heartbeat is coming back, so he goes to climb the trees,
The air brushing against him.
Jumping down he munches on his banana making a loud smacking
Sound with his lips,
Then you hear him chatter.
But wait, hearing the screech again makes him jump back in fear,
It's coming closer and closer and closer, *argh!*
The eagle sways by picking him up by one of his hairs,
The monkey is taken away up into the air until you can see it no longer.
It's *gone, gone, gone, gone, gone.*

Andrea Hakim   (9)
St Mary's School, Hampstead

Cheetah

Cheetah, cheetah, here and then there,
Running, running wherever it cares,
Here and then there.

A great mass of spots on yellow,
Quicker than a hare,
When it's over here,
Where, where,
Oh, now it is over there.

Cheetah, cheetah,
Softer than a hare,
Not quite a cheetah but nearly there.

Dashing down the African plain,
Oh no, a hunter with a gun,
Hopefully the cheetah will run, run, run.

Bunny Love Dorrell   (9)
St Mary's School, Hampstead

A Horse

There are lots of different kinds of them,
They're soft warm things, long manes, long tails,
They eat apples, carrots and oats.
They are very fast animals,
Only if they are racehorses.
'Apples and carrots are my favourite meal.
Yum-yum in my tum and then for a delicious desert,
Polos and sugar lumps.'

Charlotte Coffey (9)
St Mary's School, Hampstead

Dolphins

He swims through the water
And jumps with a wonderfully curved back
The setting sun shines on his sleek back
And glistens with sparkles of water drops.
As he swims through the water
A fishing net grabs him
So he starts to struggle but manages to get free.

Katie O'Keeffe (9)
St Mary's School, Hampstead

Alfie

Alfie is a horse,
He really likes apples,
He's really naughty and cheeky,
But I like him all the same.
Alfie is a nice horse,
And if you were with me,
You would believe me.

Gabriella Diaferia (9)
St Mary's School, Hampstead

The Cheetah

A cheetah is a wondrous animal
With sleek and spotted fur,
Prowling along the dark green grass
Without causing a stir.

With long slim legs and silent feet
It sprints among the trees,
Faster than any animal on land
Or in the seas.

Pointy teeth and sharp are its claws
Used to pounce upon its prey,
Carries it up a long dark tree
Eating as it lays.

A cheetah is a wondrous animal
With sleek and spotted fur,
Prowling along the dark green grass
Without causing a stir.

Michelle Karlsson (9)
St Mary's School, Hampstead

Tortoise

I'm in the dark,
A stranger passes by with a bark,
I tuck my head in and I wait,
I think I'm going to be ate,
But everyone thinks that I am a green stone,
I don't care, but then I groan,
I nibble a bit of lettuce
And I walk, I do not walk my fastest.
I don't wear socks,
I walk to the rocks
And there lays
A beautiful tortoise!

Jessie Chan (8)
St Mary's School, Hampstead

Ellie The Elephant

Ellie the elephant rode along,
A smile on her face
At an incredibly fast pace,
For she went out to dinner
With her mum and mate.

She had a very fun time.
The next day she was a writer
And wrote a good rhyme.

She published her book
And then became an artist.
She went to France
And drew a dance.

That was the life of Ellie
And now she's just a mummy.

Daisy Francis (9)
St Mary's School, Hampstead

My Animal

Fierce as a tiger,
Yellow or black.

It shows if it is happy,
Helpful as a dolphin purring.

Sleeping,
Scratching,
Purring and running about.

It's kind in its way,
Bringing you presents every day.

It is . . .

Kiki Biggs (9)
St Mary's School, Hampstead

My Cuddly Octopus

Octopus, octopus, cuddly as can be,
Fluffy and coloured just for me.
You're as wobbly as jelly,
You've got four pairs of wellies
And that's a lot as you can see.
So if you ever see an octopus
As cuddly as can be,
Then you know that, that octopus
Has always lived with me.

Mona Hickey (9)
St Mary's School, Hampstead

Tiger, Tiger

It looks like a teddy,
It has scary eyes,
It's all stripy and it prowls through the night,
It's very cute, it's so furry and sweet,
When it growls you will jump out of your feet.
It's a tiger, so watch out when you're out,
Don't be a lout on a dark, dark night.

Cecilia Tyrrell (9)
St Mary's School, Hampstead

Rabbit

It feels so soft
And looks so nice,
You want to cuddle it up
And squeeze or squish it,
You can't, you don't want to hurt it.
Live in a forest, well most of them do,
Some with us 'cause we love them, we do.

Amelia Seifalian (9)
St Mary's School, Hampstead

Fish

What's that over there
In the ocean swimming?
Is it a shark or is it a snail?
No it's a fish swimming over there!

It is red with shining scales,
The scales shining all over.
It is finned and scaled quite nicely
As he swims to a clover.

I feel like jumping in the ocean,
Swimming with the fish.
I would be in paradise there,
Oh, how I wish!

So I jump into the ocean
Clothes and all,
There I am free and happy,
I feel like I'm in the Queen's hall!

Charlotte Dougall (9)
St Mary's School, Hampstead

My Fluffy Friend

Soft and pure with wonderful habits,
Down in the field lays the beautiful rabbit,
Looking for food but does not have much luck.
I'm looking at him longingly, I want him so much.

It hops onto something it sees in the grass,
Something that seems much more precious than brass.
Wow! It's a carrot,
What a lucky old rabbit.

Eloise Donovan (9)
St Mary's School, Hampstead

My Puppy

Her fur is yellow and her nose is black,
She has a nice, fluffy puppy coat,
She snuggles and licks me all the time
And at night she calls to me in a howl.
She eats round dog food and drinks lots of water,
She sleeps in a crate with a nice warm blanket.
What is she?
My puppy, Maggie!

Katherine Lampard (10)
St Mary's School, Hampstead

Elephant

Splish, splash,
Trot, trot, trot
Out the water
I trip, trop, trip.
Big and grey
And dirty like a pig.
Slow, steady and big.
I love you all the same,
My friend, the elephant.

Millie Barber (9)
St Mary's School, Hampstead

The Hamster

The hamster sleeps when everyone is awake
And plays when everyone is sleeping.
He chews and climbs until the morning,
Then it is his bedtime again.
And he goes on and on living his life,
Climbing and chewing all night long.

Phoebe Mallett (9)
St Mary's School, Hampstead

A Big Cat

In a cage
Next to me,
King of the jungle
Just let him be.

Razor-sharp teeth,
Bright yellow hair,
A lovely fur necklace,
It gives me a scare.

Sitting there watching
This great roaring king,
Now I understand
This giant of a thing.

Iona Nicolson (10)
St Mary's School, Hampstead

Cats

Velvet soft fur,
    Piercing green eyes,
It looks like a sleeping tiger when it lies.

Jumping up high,
    Purring aloud,
It's like a flying hawk when it prowls.

Clawing the mice,
    Running from the dogs,
It looks very happy next to the burning logs.

Constance Osborne (9)
St Mary's School, Hampstead

Zip Wire

Up the tower, the very tall tower,
My heart thumping like a drum.
I'm at the top behind the safety barrier,
'Next,' calls the instructor.
The barrier opens,
I stand on a box,
A wobbly wooden box
And look down nervously.
I turn round shivering.
'All clear,' shouts the man.
'All clear,' shouts the other.
I am going to do an angel fall,
Ah, ah! the wind, oh glorious breeze,
Faster and faster. It's like a dead end.
Stop! I drop a black rope, unbuckle myself,
Break the penguin's neck.
Gently lifted down,
Smelling the cold air,
Smile happily,
I'd done it, I'd done the zip wire.

Ruby Mercer (9)
St Peter's Primary School, Hammersmith

Zip Wire

As I fly through the air, everything is left behind me.
I clench my fists together and yodel like a maniac Indian.

The gentle breeze sways to and fro
and I swing rapidly like a chimpanzee.

The height is daring, though impressive
and my heart burns as the rope scorches my fingertips.

My eyes squint and a smirk appears suddenly on my rosy-red cheeks.
The harness clicks and trembling I'm back on the ground.

Lily Biddell (9)
St Peter's Primary School, Hammersmith

Mud, Glorious Mud!

We came to the woods,
with the glorious smell of countryside,
I jumped and splashed with mountains of mud
toppling over me, squidgy, squishy and cold,
the feeling was so fantastic!
      That's my life!
Climbing and balancing on tyres and wood,
climbing up ropes and having mud fights,
the lovely feeling of dough (but better!)
      That's my life!
I commando-crawled under tyres,
making myself even more muddy.
Then a flash of TV came into my mind,
and I thought I'd make myself tall, Marge Simpson's hair!
      That's my life!
Last but not least, we filled our piggles hoods with mud and water,
then each of us poured it over our heads!
You can imagine that cold feeling like a bucket of ice cubes
getting spilt down your neck!
      That's my life!

Babette Van Gerwen (9)
St Peter's Primary School, Hammersmith

It's A Challenge

It's a challenge to get out of bed to go to the challenge
Because I wasn't ready to get wet and cold.

After breakfast I thought,
Am I ready for this? The answer was no!

It was a challenge to put on the cold, muddy clothes,
They get all my clothes dirty,
Was I ready for this? The answer was no!

But when I jumped into the mud pool
And felt myself sliding through the mud,
I knew I was ready. 'Whooo!'

Sam Eccles (10)
St Peter's Primary School, Hammersmith

Squelch, Squish, Splash!

Me and my mate Babs
Were squilching, squelching
In the stinking mud.
Yeah!
That's the life for me.
We kicked and splashed,
Oooooooh!
How good is that.
We swam and rolled
In dirty water.
Amazing! Fabulous! Magnificent!
Glorious! Excellent!
Whahoo! Yeah!
Now this was fun.
Then we crawled through tyres
Trying to keep mud hairstyles on our head.
Mine was a sloppy one,
That's why mine fell off.

Megan Gerrard (9)
St Peter's Primary School, Hammersmith

Zip Wire

There I was standing at the top of the zip wire
Feeling very scared, my friends were cheering me on,
My eyes went all funny, it was all very puzzling,
Should I do it or should I go down the stairs again?
And of course, I went down the stairs.
Soon it was my go again.
I decided to give it a try,
So I got up the stairs and got tied in.
I wanted to go down at the very last minute,
But next I found myself zipping down the wire,
I felt so good about myself.

Ngozi Diamond (9)
St Peter's Primary School, Hammersmith

The Challenge

I was in Year 5 and I was at PGL,
It was my 3rd activity of the second day,
'It' was the challenge course.
I felt excited as we approached a clearing in the forest,
Before me I saw the most amazing climbing frame I had ever seen,
I felt a buzz go up my body.
I stepped onto the first challenge;
A plank of wood as thin as matchsticks,
I walked carefully like a thief in the night,
I stepped onto the tyres that wobbled like jelly
And were as slimy as a toad.
I was proud when I finished
But I still had to tackle a plank of wood as low as a Dachshund.
When I got up I felt mud trickle down my chest,
I could feel the gritty taste of mud in my mouth,
My ears were also clogged with small bits of grit.
When we had finished in the water
We had to wriggle commando style through a sea of rubber tyres,
It was like being in the army.
Now we had to race through a slanted wall of rope.
All these challenges were great fun,
It was the best activity there.

Sam Smith (9)
St Peter's Primary School, Hammersmith

Mud - The Challenge Course

Mud was climbing up my sleeves
Mud was oozing in my shoes
Mud was sleeping in my hair
Mud was caked upon my face
Mud was attacking my leg.

Mud!

Emma Grace (9)
St Peter's Primary School, Hammersmith

Abseiling

I put on my hat, harness too
And got told what to do.
Then we wait, it's my go!
What do I do?
I have to go
Climbing up the ladders.
I get told to wait.
Me and my bud
We wait a few minutes
Then I climb up the last ladder,
There I go.
I get strapped up
Then start to lean back,
Aarrgghh!
So I start walking down
Then the instructor
Says, *'Jump.'*
I do it, lots of them
And then I get to the bottom,
I yell,
'I want to do it again.'

Keri Rothwell-Douglas (9)
St Peter's Primary School, Hammersmith

Furious Fencing

F ighting with swords is something I love to do
E xcitement is the feeling I get when I start a fight
N othing compares to the thrill of fencing
C oncentration is needed to win a battle
I ntense wounds are made as the swords are slashed
N obody can defend the instructor's killing blows
G loves are the items I use to challenge my opponent.

Obi Raphael (9)
St Peter's Primary School, Hammersmith

The Zip Wire

As I walk to the zip wire with my group,
When I put on my harness and helmet too,
My heart is pounding, my pulse is racing. This is exciting!

While I'm on the bench with my class,
As I watch my first mate disappear up the tower,
My heart is pounding, my pulse is racing. This is exciting!

When I see my friend getting ready,
While I watch her as she flies down the wire,
My heart is pounding, my pulse is racing. This is exciting!

As I see all the others do the same,
I wonder how wonderful it must be,
My heart is pounding, my pulse is racing. This is exciting!

When I realise my turn has finally come,
I find myself suddenly nervous,
My heart is pounding, my pulse is racing. But it's exciting!

I am on the wire, I feel like I'm flying!
My heart is pounding, my pulse is racing. And it's exciting!

Leila Tompkins (9)
St Peter's Primary School, Hammersmith

Zip Wire At Marchants Hill

Challenge course was good
Quad biking better
But zip ruled
It was so cool
It made me scream
So Marchants Hill, you get my vote
You're better than the rest
But I have to say, 'Zip wire is the best!'

Jack Gibbon (9)
St Peter's Primary School, Hammersmith

I Love The Zip Wire

Put on my harness,
Put on my hat,
Wait in the queue
Until it's my turn.

Lots of chatter,
Lots of noise,
It's my turn,
Climb up the stairs, hold on tight.

It's high up here,
I'm feeling really scared.
Sit on the box,
Clip on the ropes,
Off I go!

I'm flying through the air,
It's fantastic,
You can see everywhere.

Nearly at the end already,
It's over so quickly.
Time to let the rope down,
Stop!
Flip back the penguin,
Push down.

When can I have another go?

Mia Fennimore Holdsworth (9)
St Peter's Primary School, Hammersmith

The Zip Wire

The zip wire was extremely scary,
At first I thought, *anyway.*
Had to jump off a tremendously high tower,
As tall as a mountain it seemed,
Terrifying!

We wore harnesses to secure ourselves,
Attached to the harness a rope linked to the wire.
The wire was slanted so it made you go faster,
Terrifying!

Suddenly it was my go!
Up the stairs I climbed to the top of the tower.
I looked down, I screamed!
The instructor told me not to worry,
Time to go!
Terrifying!

I held my breath, counted to three and jumped!
Down the wire I flew, down, down, down.
Everything zooming past me, feeling dizzy.
I heard a roar of chanting saying, 'Iona! Iona!'
I had done it!
Sensational!

Iona Stirling (9)
St Peter's Primary School, Hammersmith

That Amazing Sensation

That amazing sensation,
When you cover yourself in mud.
That amazing sensation,
When you sail down the abseiling tower.

That amazing sensation,
When you release that arrow.
That amazing sensation,
When you race around that track, on a quad bike.

That amazing sensation,
When you climb through the web.
That amazing sensation,
When you explore the forest.

But the best thing of all
Is when you fly along that zip wire,
Feeling like the bottom of your stomach's dropped out,
Wow, those amazing sensations.

Rosie Morgan (9)
St Peter's Primary School, Hammersmith

Quad Biking

Quad biking, quad biking
I felt a very funny thing
It smelt like an auto stink
Petrol fumes, dust, smoke
I had my feet flat on the sides
My fingers were on the brakes
I had to avoid falling off
I crashed into a wall
I could see normally through the goggles
I felt I could do it but it turned out harder.

Louis Earle (9)
St Peter's Primary School, Hammersmith

Marchants Hill - The Inside Story

Chug, chug, chug
There we were, finally at the land of zip wire and other activities!
We were herded into a group and reunited with our luggage
A person called Amber introduced herself to us
We found our dorms and then we unpacked
Tarzan was swingin' on a rubber band
That's what we were singing on the way to orienteering
We couldn't find '21' but we knew what the words spelt
'Initiative exercises' were next, they were great!

Time for bed, well we didn't sleep for another three hours
Thanks to Megs

Climbing up the zip wire tower was dead scary!
After lunch, the challenge course
Mud oozing out of my shoes
Finally a goodnight's sleep
Kapow! Miss! That's what I'm like with a bow and arrow
Brum!
After quad bikes - home.
Chug, chug, chug
Home again!

Wallis Gray (9)
St Peter's Primary School, Hammersmith

The Zip Wire

At action-packed PGL I went abseiling
It wasn't hazardous but it was hair-raising
I had an advantage because I like freaky and fascinating things
It was exhilarating and extraordinary
It was big and breathtaking
It was terrific and terrifying
I twirled and whirled
And then I landed on the ground with a pound!
Thud!

Edward Thorpe-Woods (9)
St Peter's Primary School, Hammersmith

Quad Biking

There was a sudden roar, then oh! It was only our teacher
                                              testing the quad!

Now here's where the story begins:

It was the last day of PGL
It was our group's turn to do quads
We got all our pads on
He started up the engine with a tremendous roar
Then it turned to a rumble
Like thunder crashing upon the floor
The first person was ready to get on
Zoom, off she went, it came to a corner
Crash, bang, she hit the side
Zoom, crash
Zoom, crash
Zoom, crash
Zoom, zoom, zoom, so close, aah crash
It was my turn
Vroom, vroom, vroom, here's the corner
Eeeek! Zoom, and another *ssssshhhhhooooo!*
And to the finish
Ssss shhhooo eeek!
Next.

Bert Azis-Clauson (9)
St Peter's Primary School, Hammersmith

The Penalty

There I was standing in the middle of the pitch,
The game started,
The crowd were crazy,
The ball rolled to me
And I passed it to Joe
And he passed it back to me.

I was in the penalty area
And I got a foul,
It was a penalty.

I shot with all my might
And it was a goal!
The crowd went wild
And said,
'Billy, Billy the kid,
Billy, Billy the kid.'

Alex Burch (10)
St Peter's Primary School, Hammersmith

Bentley

Red Bentley.
Shiny red Bentley.
It will be 'first in a race' Bentley.
Excellent car.
Very, very, very, very good.
Nice and beautiful Bentley.
Very sexy Bentley.
'Very nice inside' Bentley.
It has a big-screen TV and a PSP.

Kane Bryant (7)
St Stephen's CE Primary School, Westminster

At The Weekend

At,
At the,
At the weekend,
At the weekend I went,
At the weekend I went to,
At the weekend I went to the,
At the weekend I went to the park,
At the weekend I went to the park next,
At the weekend I went to the park next to,
At the weekend I went to the park next to my,
At the weekend I went to the park next to my house,
At the weekend I went to the park next to my house and,
At the weekend I went to the park next to my house and I,
At the weekend I went to the park next to my house and I played,
At the weekend I went to the park next to my house and I played on,
At the weekend I went to the park next to my house and I played on the
S
   L
     I
       D
         E.

Timor Saleh (7)
St Stephen's CE Primary School, Westminster

Bus Stop

I can hear a noise,
What is that noise?
I am squashed because there are a lot of people,
The bus is full,
The bus stops,
People are coming inside,
The bus goes again,
Finally it is my stop,
I hop off and walk home.

Ismail Taibi (7)
St Stephen's CE Primary School, Westminster

Where Am I?

I can see the nursery,
I can see the TV,
I can hear the fire alarm,
I can see a radio,
I can see the benches,
I can see the gym,
I can smell perfume,
I can see chairs,
I can see the mat,
I can see the dinosaur wall,
I can hear footsteps,
I can see a piano,
I can see the door,

Where am I?

In the Infant Hall.

Zeynab Mohamed (7)
St Stephen's CE Primary School, Westminster

Where Am I?

I see a guitar,
I can hear Amie talking,
I can see Lily-May copying,
I can see Rron moving,
I can hear my teacher whispering,
I can see some legs,
I can see coats,
I can see a door with a sign saying *Fire Exit.*

Where am I?

In the classroom.

Lulu James (7)
St Stephen's CE Primary School, Westminster

Where Am I?

I hear people talking,
I hear people walking,
I hear people working,
I see books,
I see a laptop,
I see a whiteboard,
I see a pen,
I see boxes,
I see a tap,
I see pencils,

Where am I?

In the classroom.

Naheeda Ahad (7)
St Stephen's CE Primary School, Westminster

The Mystery

I am the follower of the master of knowledge,
I am the pointy claw of the lion that protects.
I am the whizz of all capitals,
I am the mouse that does not make a sound,
I am the collage of the perfect artist,
I am the magma that can burn.

Who is the spear that never gives up?
Who is the writer of similes?
Who is the kindest of the friends?

(If not I?)

Tahera Bahar (9)
St Stephen's CE Primary School, Westminster

Where Am I?

I see benches,
I see tables and children,
I see chairs,
I hear children moving,
I see food on the tables,
I see cups on the tables,
I see the door,
I see my friend Rron,
I see the sun,
I hear children outside playing,
I hear cars outside,
I see my friend Timor,
I see my friends,
I see the wall.

Where am I?

In the dinner hall.

Karan Jeantilal (7)
St Stephen's CE Primary School, Westminster

Where Am I?

I hear chairs moving,
I can hear people typing,
I can hear people whispering,
I can hear someone shutting the door,
I can see people walking around,
I can see a teacher closing the window.

Where am I?

In the computer room.

Iftekhar Boksh (7)
St Stephen's CE Primary School, Westminster

Silly Kelly

A silly girl named Kelly,
always wore
a bright red welly.
And on her left
It always stayed.
And on her right
a trainer remained.
She wore them
every day and night.
Everybody got a fright
for one stormy,
thunder-bolting night,
she turned into a
king-sized kite!

Imani McKoy (9)
St Stephen's CE Primary School, Westminster

Where Am I?

I can hear people splashing in the water,
I can feel the sun burning my body,
I can see people lying on the little shells,
I can hear people playing in the blue water,
I can hear people chewing bubblegum,
I can hear people licking ice cream.

Where am I?

At the beach.

Nora Zejnullahi (7)
St Stephen's CE Primary School, Westminster

Where Am I?

I can hear the waves splashing,
I can see sandcastles,
I can smell salty water,
I can taste an ice cream,
I can see children splashing,
I can hear my dad calling me,
I can taste yummy food,
I can hear children screaming,
I can see children putting the shells on their sandcastles,
I can taste another ice cream.

Where am I?

At the beach at Bournemouth.

Marineke Canavan (7)
St Stephen's CE Primary School, Westminster

Where Am I?

I hear birds singing,
I hear cows mooing,
I hear ducks quacking,
I see ponies and horses,
I see grass and flowers,
I see rocks and stones.

Where am I?

At the farm.

Lily-May Allcock (7)
St Stephen's CE Primary School, Westminster

At The Weekend

At,
At the,
At the weekend,
At the weekend I,
At the weekend I walked,
At the weekend I walked to,
At the weekend I walked to the,
At the weekend I walked to the shop,
At the weekend I walked to the shop with,
At the weekend I walked to the shop with my,
At the weekend I walked to the shop with my mum.

Munkhdul Batsukh (7)
St Stephen's CE Primary School, Westminster

Where Am I?

I hear a teacher shouting,
I see people swing on chairs,
I hear pencils going on the floor,
I see books swishing open,
I hear people mumbling,
I hear my friends laughing,
I hear people talking,
I see a window,
I can hear the wind swishing in my hair,
I see the blue sky.

Where am I?

In the classroom.

Sian Garett (7)
St Stephen's CE Primary School, Westminster

The Mystery

I am a swirling tornado.
I am as fast as a cheetah.
I am a lighting storm that strikes every day.
I am a sword in battle that strikes every day.
I am a good friend that protects my friends like a shield.

Who is it that is a cheetah
hunting for food?

Who is it that is as angry
as a lightning storm?

Who is it that is as talented
as an athletic runner,

(If not I ?)

Tariq Jobson (9)
St Stephen's CE Primary School, Westminster

At The Weekend

At,
At the,
At the weekend,
At the weekend my,
At the weekend my cousin,
At the weekend my cousin and,
At the weekend my cousin and I,
At the weekend my cousin and I went,
At the weekend my cousin and I went to,
At the weekend my cousin and I went to the,
At the weekend my cousin and I went to the shops.

Ishrath Iqbal (7)
St Stephen's CE Primary School, Westminster

Where Am I?

I can hear people running in the playground,
I can hear the teachers speaking,
It is very dark,
I can smell chips,
I can hear children talking,
I can hear sirens,
I can still hear teachers speaking,
Now it's gone a bit quieter,
I can hear children's books,
I can still hear the teacher speaking,
I can see children and teacher,
I can hear a person speaking,
I can hear the teacher speaking,
It is getting darker,
I see people going to the toilet,
I can see the blue sky,
I can see and hear people speaking,
I am really uncomfortable,
It is really cold,
I can hear the wind blowing,
I can hear someone saying, 'What are you doing?'
I can hear people going up the stairs,
I can see the teacher walking,
I can hear people coughing.

Where am I?

On the stairwell.

Khadiza Akther (7)
St Stephen's CE Primary School, Westminster

The Mystery

I am as colourful
     as a rainbow

I am a sun
     with all the
     brightness

I am as loud
     as the storm
     falling down

I am a younger brother
     who's kind
     to others.

Who has the shot of
     power?

Who has the brain of
     maths?

Who shines out as the
     sun up
     above

(If not I?)

Adonay Yemane (9)
St Stephen's CE Primary School, Westminster

The Mystery

I am a tornado that strikes every day.
I am a baby full of rivers.
I am a bird that tweets every day in the morning but never seen.
I am a clever book with excellent words inside.
I am a snail racing to a tall tree.
I am a shield in battle all alone.
I am a hilarious clown.

(If not I ?)

Lina Ishak (9)
St Stephen's CE Primary School, Westminster

The Mystery

I am a tree that stands up proud,
I am an erupting volcano that spits out ash,
I am a ball that blasts into the goal,
I am a rhino that charges into walls,
I am a sun that shines our love,
I am a shield of protection,
I am a drill that shouts out love,
I am a cheetah that chases its prey,
I am a sword in battle,
I am a monkey that climbs up trees,
I am a word of science,
I am a leader that leads Mini Rebels into victory,
So who is it that has the skills of Ronaldinho?
Who is it that has friends, a lot of friends?

(If not I?)

Isaac Johnson (9)
St Stephen's CE Primary School, Westminster

The Unknown Human

I am a snake that has no trouble.
I am a dinosaur with incredible strength.
I am a blowing wind that brushes past you.
I am a tsunami that washes you away.
I am a supernova that destroys the world around you.
I am the book that contains continuous knowledge.

Who is it that sneaks upon you?
Who is it that is as fearless as a knight?

(If not I?)

Nahid Ahmed (9)
St Stephen's CE Primary School, Westminster

The Mystery

I am as long-sighted as an eagle
I am as good at reading as a professor
I am a turtle struggling to keep up
I am a star that brightens my family's life
I am the ocean spray irritating a sailor
I am a radar that has broken down
I am a ticket to go first.

Who is it that has two nieces?
Who is it that has two brothers, 27 years old?
Who is it that goes to the choir.

(If not I?)

Marco Tripalo (10)
St Stephen's CE Primary School, Westminster

The Wonder

I hear the whistle of the wind,
so soft and gentle, not even knowing that it's there.
I can feel the beam of the sun,
so warm and loving, it's like it cares.
I can see the rain,
dripping on my face like tears of shame.
Where do you think these come from?
The wind, the rain and the sun.
Over none. It is one.

Salma Dahdouh (10)
St Stephen's CE Primary School, Westminster

The Mystery

I am a supporter that helps people when they're stuck,
I am a radio that talks like parrots,
I am a tornado that can blow cars,
I am a lion that protects people.

Who is it that learns a lot?
Who is it that helps people when they are stuck?
Who is it that cares about people?

(If not I?)

Shamima Aktar (9)
St Stephen's CE Primary School, Westminster

The Hippo And The Field Mouse

The hippo and the field mouse
Went to America
On a National Express coach
They took some sweet honey and plenty of money
And some sheepskin coats.

Hippo said to the mouse,
'My gosh, what a nice house,
How beautiful can you sing?'
The coach went down to town,
And the mobile phone went *ring, ring!*

'Dear Hippo, you sing very well
But how about we do a show?'
'My dear, you couch potato, what about our video?
I haven't seen 'The X-Factor' but I shall certainly give it a go!'

Shahed Ali (9)
Sir William Burrough Primary School, Limehouse

The Lion And The Tiger

The lion and the tiger went on a walk
On the crusty, rusty leaves they saw
A witch, so wicked she was
Always breaking the law.

'Oh witch, oh witch,' said the tiger
'Who is best dressed of all?'
'Not you two,' laughed the witch
As she clambered over the wall.

She clambered over the wall, her pointy nose got stuck
She pulled her nose, it started to bleed
She pulled it more, it got worse, she was under a curse
She was so happy when it was finally freed.

Mim Ahmed (9)
Sir William Burrough Primary School, Limehouse

The Pony And The Rabbit

The pony and the rabbit went to Bangladesh
By climbing onto a pogo stick,
They took their parrots and plenty of carrots
But all they wanted to do were tricks

The pony said to the rabbit,
'My goodness, I think we've had it!
How are we going to get there?
But to tell the truth, I don't really care.'

They had their rest, put on their vest and said,
'Let's do a Paula Radcliffe!'
Off they shot into a water pot
And never got out of the lift.

Arefa Tahiya Uddin (8)
Sir William Burrough Primary School, Limehouse

The Donkey And The Table

The donkey and the table went to China
In a bright red coach.
They took a table and a bagel
As the bagel was poached.

Donkey said to the table, 'You flat thing,'
While Big Ben went *ring, ding, dong, ding!*
And his ear went dark red
In a few minutes flat
He forgot about that and felt sick and went to bed

'Dear Piggy, give me your owner Milly
And let me sell her for five pounds.'
They got five shillings and thought they'd made a killing
And gave the piggy a mud bath in the ground.

Hana Lam (9)
Sir William Burrough Primary School, Limehouse

The Cat And The Mouse

The cat and the mouse went to Sweden
On a giant boat.
They took some cheese and bees
To sell for a nice little coat.

When they arrived in Sweden,
They got their coats,
Some monkeys and donkeys
And swapped them for a goat.

The cat and the mouse went back home
In their sports car.
They took money and a baby bunny
To give to their ma.

Amelia Clark (8)
Sir William Burrough Primary School, Limehouse

The Peacock And The Kangaroo

The peacock and the kangaroo went to China
On colourful, bouncy pogo sticks
They took some flour and plenty of power
As they loved to play magic tricks

They stole some dough and plenty of jam
To make some Angel Delight
For a girl who liked to twirl
With eyes so very bright

The girl gave the peacock and kangaroo some advice,
'Why not make some more for your friends?'
'We have no jam but plenty of lamb.'
'Then I'll have to sell my contact lens.'

Li Cheung (8)
Sir William Burrough Primary School, Limehouse

A Poor Girl In Victorian Times

My name is Helena.
I am a poor Victorian child,
My mum and dad send me to work.
I have never been to school,
I work in a factory,
I am twelve years old.
I feel sick, tired and dizzy all the time,
I feel like I am just about to faint.
I want to go to school but I can't,
We have no money.
I have to work,
If I am late for work,
They beat me up!
When am I going to leave work?
There is all darkness around me.
I smell horrible smoke.
I am really scared.
I am shivering,
Please someone, help!

Soner Doldur (10)
Thomas Fairchild Community School, Hackney

A Poor Victorian Child

My name is Alice
And I am seven years old.
I work in a mine, it is a factory,
I feel cold, sleepy.
I can see nothing,
My eyes are blurry.
Blood drops from my hands,
I feel devastated, dizzy and worried.
My hands are weak, I feel sleepy,
There's nothing but darkness around me,
I'm just about to faint!
I have clothes that are ripped,
And I feel smelly,
There's nothing that I can do
Except keep working . . .

                Love from Krystal.

Krystal Ruth Brown
Thomas Fairchild Community School, Hackney

The Big Bang

                In the galaxy
                There was nothing.
                In the middle of nowhere.
                In the galaxy.

There was a big bang!
Out came the sun,
And some stars.
Then Mercury, Venus, Earth, Mars,
Jupiter, Neptune, Uranus and Pluto.

Some more stars came.

                In zillions of years it will be gone forever!
                        Or forever not!

Carim Akeju (9)
Thomas Fairchild Community School, Hackney

My Victorian Poem

My name is Beatrice
And I am a poor Victorian child,
I feel sick and
I work in a factory.
I am seven years old.
I feel worried and terrified.
I feel cold and shivery.
I smell lots of rubbish around me.
I smell smoke and horrible things.
I see darkness around me.
No lights.
My eyes are blurry,
My head feels dizzy.
I am tired.
I see ripped clothes and I feel sad.
I wear ripped clothes and feel smelly.
I have to keep working.

Yonca Belliki (9)
Thomas Fairchild Community School, Hackney

Sun, Earth, Moon

The sun, Earth and moon are in space.
It's a big space which has no gravity.
It is pitch-black.
It's got millions of stars,
Even near Mars.
It's so pretty,
But what a pity that we can't reach it.
It's bigger than a sandpit.
Bigger than a packed lunch kit
And something that you can't knit.
The sun is big,
Not the same colour as a pig.
The moon is made out of rock,
That really gives me a shock!

Silan Fidan (9)
Thomas Fairchild Community School, Hackney

I'm Suffering . . .

I'm working in a factory.
I'm injured . . .
All over!
I can see rich children playing.
I feel angry, worn-out shivery and cold!
I feel like fainting and crying.
I'm terrified to death.
I'm weak and frustrated.
I don't know what to do!
I'm fed up.
I'm leaving.
No, I'm not.
I'm staying.
Oh I don't know what to do.
My hands ache.
I feel like dying.
The Earth is shaking!
My head is shaking!
I'm suffering!

Claire Bywater (9)
Thomas Fairchild Community School, Hackney

Sun And Earth

Earth:
The Earth is a big round ball.
The Earth is made out of water and land.
The Earth has an Equator,
The Equator is a long line
That goes through the Earth.

Sun:
The sun is a big flaming star
That sits in the sky.
It's a bright star,
That will blind you
If you look at it.

Manuel Decasas (9)
Thomas Fairchild Community School, Hackney

And My Heart Thumps

Working in a mine
Hitting and shoving
Working 24/7
I'm only seven
Help me! Please!

The hardness of the walls
Hitting and shoving
Pushing and pulling
That's all I do.

Every day I see blood
And there's sometimes a flood
Blood falling and dripping
Aching and hurting.

All I hear is
Clank! Clank! Clank!
Bump, bump!
Every day
This way and that,
And my heart thumps.

Winnie Mac (9)
Thomas Fairchild Community School, Hackney